CHILD LIBERATION SERIES: BOOK 1

THE SOUND OF FREEDOM

True Stories that Inspired the Film

*"I will do everything in my power to eradicate
this evil from the face of the earth!"*

PAUL HUTCHINSON

ISBN: 978-1-960346-23-0 (Hardback)
ISBN: 978-1-960346-24-7 (Paperback)
ISBN: 978-1-960346-25-4 (Ebook)

Authorsunite.com

This book is a memoir. It reflects the author's present recollections of experiences over time. Some names and characteristics have been changed, some events have been compressed, and some dialogue has been recreated.

DEDICATION

"What we do in life echoes in eternity."
~ Marcus Aurelius ~

This book is dedicated to the *Hidden Heroes*—those courageous men and women who risked everything to secure a future where children can thrive in freedom. It is an immense honor to have stood shoulder-to-shoulder with some of the finest undercover operators the world has known.

These remarkable individuals bravely ventured into dangerous places, risking everything to find and save those who couldn't speak up for themselves. They weren't motivated by fame or money but fought tirelessly for the defenseless, going into the shadows where others dared not go.

Even the victims they rescued often didn't know about these heroes who risked their lives for their freedom. Many of these heroes continue their undercover work, tirelessly freeing children from the clutches of evil. Their courage has earned my deepest respect, and I am forever grateful for the privilege of serving alongside them.

This book also pays tribute to every parent, grandparent, sibling, educator, mentor, and friend who works to heal, love, and protect the children in our world. As we unite to liberate humanity, your courage and unwavering resolve become a light of hope that inspires the world. In your noble effort to preserve innocence, may you lead with infinite compassion and unconditional love. Let us collectively pray for the day when every child can joyously proclaim their own *Sound of Freedom.*

CONTENTS

PART I:
THE MAKING OF AN UNDERCOVER OPERATOR

PART II:
THE ISLAND

PART III:
UNDERCOVER ALIAS - DOCTORS IN THE JUNGLE

PART IV:
LIBERATING HUMANITY FROM SLAVERY

FOREWORD

If we do not protect our future generations, we will have nothing left to live for. Dedicating our lives to protecting our children is not just a wise choice but an absolute obligation if we want to see our world become a better place for all. My dear friend, Paul Hutchinson, has fulfilled this obligation, risking everything in the process, including both his private life and professional career. He did not have to do any of it, however, he chose to in honor of protecting our future generations, our children. Although what you are about to read is heart-wrenching, becoming aware of the true horrors of our world is the first step that must be taken to transmute darkness into Light. From this perspective, it is inspiring.

Paul Hutchinson has encountered the darkness that lurks in the shadows of our world today. He has been face-to-face with the very people responsible for some of the most heinous crimes imaginable. As he shared his stories with me first-hand, with undeniable pictures and videos to prove his case, I asked him, "Why did you do it?", His response was, "Because what kind of man would I be if I just kept living my luxurious life while children around the world were being raped, tortured, and murdered, and I did nothing about it knowing very well that I could do something to change it?". With tears in my eyes, that was the moment I knew that Paul needed to be supported in every way, shape, and form.

That is why I, along with the EESystem team, decided to invest in the blockbuster hit, *Sound of Freedom,* against all advisory and consultation, telling us that we would completely lose our investment. The investment in the film was not done with the intention of making money but rather to bring awareness to a priceless story that the world needed to become aware of, and that is exactly what happened. It became apparent to me that with unwavering courage and unyielding determination, Paul and his team have dedicated themselves to the cause of rescuing trafficked children from the clutches of exploitation and despair while receiving nothing in return other than the fulfillment of positively impacting their lives. Through their tireless efforts, thousands of lives have been saved, and countless futures have been restored.

In the following pages that you are about to read, Paul offers a deep reflection on his upbringing and how he acquired the skills essential to his undercover child rescue missions. From there, he tells his journey of amassing wealth by establishing a multibillion-dollar enterprise only to risk everything to venture into the most dangerous places on the planet for the sake of saving the children caught in trafficking. As we are guided through the abyss of human wickedness, Paul ultimately leads us back to the liberating warmth of reclaiming our collective freedom. As you immerse yourself in the horrific accounts and uplifting triumphs contained within these pages, may you be inspired to join the fight for helping to heal humanity once and for all.

Your way may be different than Paul's, but every way on this path is needed to overcome darkness and reclaim the Light. After all, it is only through collective action and unwavering solidarity that we can truly create a world where every child is free to live a life of dignity, safety, and opportunity. This story is a powerful witness to the fact that each of us possesses unique talents capable of combating the evils in this world and how, together, we can create positive change in our future. Prepare to be moved, prepare to be challenged, and prepare to be inspired. The journey you are about to experience is not merely a story… it is a call to action, a call for justice, and a call for hope. May you be blessed to hear this call and take proper action.

Love,
Jason Shurka

INTRODUCTION

A single spark can ignite a flame that illuminates the entire universe. A single moment can set in motion a movement that liberates millions of children and heals humanity—such a moment in history occurred on a secluded island off the coast of Colombia on October 13, 2014. Invited to play a pivotal role in an undercover operation, I became part of a mission that liberated over one hundred victims that day. As we unraveled the evil plans of child traffickers, the heart-wrenching cries of children tore at our hearts.

Following the successful sting operation, the aftercare team swiftly moved in to begin the long and delicate process of healing the children's emotional scars. As we prepared to leave the scene, the air filled with an unexpected and beautiful sound—laughter and singing from the liberated victims. The song of children's joy brought unimaginable joy to our hearts.

"That Sound of Freedom was the most
beautiful melody I have ever heard."

At that moment, it was a song of victory, a choir of happiness, and a potent reminder of why we keep going. Their clear, powerful voices penetrated our souls deeply, reinforcing our commitment to this cause. We knew the story of their freedom could shine a light on the darkest part of humanity.

As you immerse yourself in the experiences and training that led to the rescue of thousands of children, I hope you will enjoy a personal transformation similar to mine. In a world filled with oppression and modern-day slavery, let us stand together in the fight for freedom.

Liberating humanity from the horrors of things such as child trafficking involves overcoming a range of challenges. It requires breaking the chains of addiction, ending cycles of domestic violence, healing from generational trauma, and lifting communities out of poverty. Let this journey inspire us to strive for a future where freedom prevails, where every child can enjoy a life unrestrained from the chains that bind them and realize their fullest potential.

In these pages, you will discover vital insights that can be used to safeguard your children and family in various situations. You will gain valuable knowledge on identifying potential risks, whether online or in your community, and learn practical strategies to enhance safety measures. You will also develop a deeper understanding of how to recognize the signs of trafficking, abuse, and other adversities that may impact people in your family or community. This awareness won't only give you the tools to protect yourself and your loved ones but also enable you to extend support and aid to those who may be vulnerable.

May this knowledge encourage you to embrace a deeper level of compassion and empathy for those suffering from childhood trauma while also revealing aspects of your personal history requiring healing. As you uncover these revelations, may fear, anger, and hatred be converted into the positive forces of faith, joy, and love, empowering you to contribute positively to the well-being of others and create a world where every child can flourish in safety and dignity.

I will never understand what drives someone to hurt a child. As guardians of innocence, we must unite and protect the children of this world. The fight for liberty and peace begins within our homes as we strive to create a healthy environment for our families to thrive. I encourage readers of this book to search within themselves and consider how they can contribute to this fight for liberation and protection. Together, through our actions, big and small, we can create a path towards a future where every child is secure, cherished, and free to realize their unlimited potential.

This book shares my firsthand experience of the real-life child rescue missions portrayed in the *Sound of Freedom* movie. The film combines narratives from various real-life child rescue operations conducted across multiple countries by skilled operatives. These stories of hundreds of operators were woven together to create a compelling storyline enacted by a small cast of actors.

Despite efforts to discredit the movie and minimize the seriousness of child trafficking, I can personally testify that the stories are true. While the screenplay took creative liberties and exaggerated the roles of some individuals, the rescue operations depicted were based on actual events. The movie draws from the combined experiences of operatives involved in over eight missions. It is designed to help the audience understand the depth of the child trafficking issue more thoroughly.

In narrating pivotal stories leading up to the undercover work and the true-life tale of the Colombian mission, I have included both the heartwarming and the horrific details, aiming to arouse in you the same emotional journey my team and I underwent. You will empathize with the children, feeling their pain and hope, and then share in their joy as they embrace the light of liberation. Every effort has been made to provide ample context while safeguarding the identities of the victims and our active operators.

A phone call from the Attorney General changed my life completely. I was invited to assume the role of a wealthy real estate mogul in an undercover operation targeting human traffickers who were constructing a child brothel. Among the 124 victims rescued, one, in particular, changed the trajectory of my path. Dubbed "Princess" by her captors, she became the focal point of the *Sound of Freedom* movie. Standing before me, tears streaming down her face, I made a solemn commitment to myself, to God, and to that little girl: I would do everything in my power to eradicate child trafficking from our world. This book is the unfolding of my journey.

PART I

THE MAKING OF AN UNDERCOVER OPERATOR

TRAINING, CHARITY, AND MONEY

1

Vigilance in the Shadows

Tactical Training to Protect Yourself and Your Family

The pounding of my heartbeat echoed in my ears, drowning out everything else. Every sense was on high alert, trying to detect the threat that could come from any direction. Standing in the center of a room with a black hood over my head, the darkness was suffocating, pressing in from all sides. The air was thick with the scent of danger, and every rustle signaled a possible threat. Racing thoughts fought for control, but training took over, calming the anxiety and sharpening the focus on the skills needed for survival.

Sweat trickled down my forehead, fists clenched, preparing for the unknown. Suddenly, the hood was yanked off, revealing a man charging forward, knife raised high. Another figure stood to the right, his presence less immediate but still threatening. In that split second, the decision was made to confront the knife-wielding attacker head-on.

Years of intense training took over, and every second mattered. Leaning into the oncoming threat, the knife thrust was blocked, and the attacker swiftly disarmed. As the first threat was neutralized, the second man lunged with a bat. Closing the gap between us, I threaded my arms between his head and the weapon and, with a swift knee to his groin, seized control of the bat.

Cheers erupted from the spectators, pulling the focus back to reality. The focus on the training had been so intense that the audience had nearly been forgotten.

Over the past twenty years, our team has attended or facilitated countless courses like this one. Each is designed to develop specific skills necessary in a dangerous situation. All of our undercover operators on child rescue missions have undergone rigorous training, either through government agencies or private programs like this. Working undercover in the world's most dangerous places demands a unique mindset, which can only be developed through intense training.

The black hood, suspended from a ceiling pulley, effectively improved our ability to assess threats and react instantly. Sharpening our senses was a vital part of the exercise. Learning to respond quickly to any threat would later save lives during child rescue missions.

Some exercises were designed to test our fighting skills, while others were intended to teach how to calm someone down using de-escalation techniques. The sudden removal of the hood forced us to analyze situations swiftly. We had to determine if the people and the environment posed a threat that needed to be neutralized or if we should try to calm the situation. Learning to disarm was valuable, but the ability to read and judge threat levels became vital during my later involvement in undercover operations.

"Fantastic job, Paul!" exclaimed one of the former Navy SEALs overseeing the training. "That was a quick response and a very effective takedown! Now, who would like to go next?"

"My turn!" declared Randy. Even though he had less training, he stepped forward eagerly.

Randy was the CEO of a successful company and had invested millions of dollars in our real estate fund. He was a close friend who would later help finance some child rescue missions in Latin America. He stood in the middle of the room as the black hood was lowered onto his head, and the former Special Forces operators set the stage for the next ambush.

One by one, the men and women tested their skills with the Navy SEALs. Most of them were new to this type of training but were eager to learn techniques that could keep them and their families safe in dangerous situations. They were business owners, real estate developers, and entrepreneurs who had reached a level of financial success that made them potential targets.

At the time, I was building an investment fund with my business partner, John Pennington. As the company grew more successful, it became clear that building client relationships was essential to the fund's growth.

"Why don't you take these potential investors golfing?" John suggested. "Most of these guys love to golf and are used to discussing business on the course."

"John, I can barely make it through a miniature golf game, let alone spend four hours driving around a country club! It's better to teach them something valuable and different, like self-defense or handling automatic weapons at a gun range," was my response. "Building relationships with these investors while teaching them practical skills that could save their lives in a dangerous situation seems more effective."

Decades of training made personal defense techniques second nature. Over the years, the operators built an impressive collection of firearms, and our children were taught to handle them safely while enjoying the art of shooting. Friends and colleagues were often invited to join in the training exercises, and many of the world's top trainers were hired to ensure that our self-defense and weapons-handling skills were continually refined and enhanced.

Many people live in continuous fear, consumed by worries ranging from finances to personal safety. In the book *7 Habits of Highly Effective People,* Steven Covey suggests that we each have a "Circle of influence" and a "Circle of concern." Most people feel helpless because they have hundreds of things in their circle of concern over which they have little influence.

A healthy way to live is to keep both circles—the circle of concern and the circle of influence—the same size. This approach meant that if something caused anxiety, there were two options: either push it out of the circle of concern and choose not to worry about it, or take the time to expand the circle of influence to address the fears and eliminate the anxiety.

Recognizing the dangers present in our world, it became clear that learning self-defense skills was essential, especially for parents. In an increasingly hazardous society, some criminals harm others to satisfy their desires for sex, money, and power. Faced with this reality, one can either ignore the threat and live in constant fear or take proactive steps to learn the necessary skills to alleviate these concerns. Prioritizing the acquisition of self-defense skills empowers people to protect themselves and their families, making it a crucial responsibility for every parent.

Our family chose to expand our circle of influence and manage potential threats by embracing personal defense and firearms training. We spent many years honing these skills. As a result, instead of showcasing poor golf skills to clients, it made more sense to invite them to join martial arts classes or head out to the desert for target practice with a .50 caliber rifle.

Few people experience the thrill of hitting a target over a mile away. Friends and clients were often surprised by the number of factors that must be considered for accuracy at such a distance. While many were aware of variables like ammunition type, wind speed, and distance, they were often surprised to learn how crucial it is to account for altitude, air temperature, barrel temperature, barometric pressure, and even the earth's rotation.

The position of your finger on the trigger and the timing of your breath can significantly impact accuracy at 1,000 yards. This experience can be compared to life, where even the most minor adjustments can have a dramatic effect on the future. We often don't need to make a complete 180-degree change; sometimes, just a few minor tweaks can significantly improve the rest of our lives.

On the way back to the city from one such shooting activity, one of the participants asked, "Paul, how do I keep my family safe while they are at school or traveling abroad? Learning to shoot a mile away is fun, but I do not think it will help with most potential threats against my kids."

"Have your children ever had any self-defense training?" I asked. "The freedom and peace of mind you gain as a parent, knowing your child can defend themselves, is priceless."

We spoke about different types of martial arts, and I suggested he consider Krav Maga. I told him, "Many types of martial arts are 'Bow to your sensei and two points when you land a successful kick to the body.' In essence, the training you receive conditions you to *avoid* deadly strikes because they are illegal in the ring."

"Any defense training is better than none, but Krav Maga is more of an unarmed, self-defense combat system than a martial art," I explained. "Krav Maga is about using whatever means necessary to survive and protect your loved ones. It's the hand-to-hand combat training of the Israeli special forces and is considered one of the most lethal systems in the world. Unlike traditional martial arts, it isn't restricted to rules designed to keep opponents safe. If you want to free your children from fear and boost their self-confidence, encourage them to learn Krav Maga."

"Wow! That sounds amazing!" he responded. How do I find a good teacher? I won't have to send my kids overseas to get decent training, will I?"

"No, actually," I responded, "Joseph, one of the world's top Krav Maga trainers, lives in our area. He is among the few qualified to return to Israel to train other trainers. I am having him come to our house for one-on-one training next week. Why don't you bring your family and see if they enjoy it?"

Twenty people came to my home the following week, eager to learn skills that would help keep their families safe. During the class orientation, Joseph taught the attendees how to overcome the fear of using force to neutralize a threat. He posed a challenging scenario to the group, asking, "If an attacker had you pinned down and was attempting to rape you or even kill you. How many of you would feel capable of defending yourselves by, for example, sticking your finger into their eye and causing permanent damage?" Only a few hands went up. Most attendees were uncomfortable with the thought of such an escalation of force.

Joseph continued, "The first step to defending yourself is being willing to match the perpetrator's aggression with an effective deterrent. It is said that everyone has a plan until they are punched in the face. Or, in this case, has their eyeball gouged out. If you are being attacked, you *must* be willing to take the steps to defend yourself and your family."

We often invited Joseph back to conduct training and teach basic self-defense to groups of friends and investors. The men learned skills to keep their families safe, and the women felt empowered, knowing they could protect themselves even if the attackers were much larger than them.

Over the years, Joseph became our steadfast protector on numerous undercover child rescue missions throughout Latin America. His expertise in Krav Maga provided unmatched security, even in the most dangerous places where children were being sold. With Joseph on the mission, our team always felt a sense of safety, confident that we could face any danger together.

Aside from teaching physical skills, Joseph and many other trainers made a critical point in our classes: "You win every fight you can avoid." No matter how much training you think you have in physical combat, if you can do things to keep your family safe *without* having to fight, then that is the very best outcome.

Never let your ego lead you into situations that could endanger you or your family. Regardless of the extent of your training or confidence level in overpowering an opponent, avoiding conflict is always the wisest course of action. The primary objective should always be to safeguard yourself and your loved ones by steering clear of potential threats whenever possible. Prioritize removing yourself and your family from any scenarios that could escalate into danger. Recognizing that prevention and caution are the most effective forms of protection is true wisdom.

Steve, one of my other trainers, refers to this point as the "Nike move," meaning "Turn the heels of your shoes to the attacker and get out of danger." He also taught how, when removing yourself from the area is not an option, the next best move is what he calls "Getting off the X." In movie making, an X is often placed on the floor so an actor knows where to stand for the best shot. In a combat situation, Steve said, "You must make moves to get yourself off the X as part of your defense, thereby moving out of the line of fire or out of the direct attack of a perpetrator."

As with most of our trainers, Steve's background is quite impressive. He has taught executives, celebrities, law enforcement, and the United States intelligence community for over thirty years. Through his improvised weapons training, our groups became efficient at neutralizing a threat using everything from a comb to a handkerchief.

While Steve is also highly respected for his edged weapons and firearms courses, his specialty is *awareness-based* training. If you want to keep your family safe, one of the most important aspects of self-defense is avoiding danger by knowing what to watch out for and how to act.

During one training session, he taught an important point: "Many criminals are insecure and tend to target people who seem like easy prey." He explained this by telling us about a study conducted in prison, where felons were shown various videos of people in public spaces and were asked to identify potential victims. "In almost every instance," he explained, "the criminals pinpointed the same people based on their behavior. Those most likely to be victimized were people who were alone, distracted, unaware of their surroundings, visibly carrying money, predictable in their actions, or displaying low self-esteem."

He taught the importance of awareness and behavioral adjustment as key strategies for avoiding potential conflicts. By remaining vigilant, staying aware of your environment, and projecting confidence, you can greatly reduce the likelihood of becoming a target. Simple changes in behavior, such as keeping your head up and your hands-free, can significantly affect personal safety.

As parents, we can't always be there to ensure the safety of our children, but we *can* decrease the chances of potential harm by arming them with a few essential tools.

Teach them to be aware of their surroundings by taking off their headphones, putting their phone away, and paying attention to the world around them. This alone will help deter potential attackers who want to catch them distracted.

Teach your kids to walk confidently, keep their heads up, and look people in the eye. Aggressors prefer victims who are timid and won't put up any resistance. Help your children understand that even if they feel fearful, simply acting confident will make a criminal think twice about attacking them.

Also, be mindful of anything you or your child is wearing that looks valuable or could be a target for theft. A criminal will weigh the risks versus rewards of attacking you. Even if you look confident and aware, they may overlook that and attempt to target you if they see enough value to outweigh the risk. Also, keep in mind that the value depends on where you are. An expensive watch or necklace might be the target in the United States, but in some third-world countries, a thief would risk a lot to steal an iPhone from you.

Labeling your child's name on their backpack might seem like a good way to keep track of their belongings, but it can make them a target for criminals. We advise parents to avoid putting their child's first name on backpacks or clothing. Predators might see the name and pretend to know the child, deceiving them into thinking they are a family friend. It's safer not to display first names or nicknames on jackets, backpacks, or other visible items. If you still want to label belongings, consider using initials instead of full names.

The buddy system is another effective strategy to enhance safety. Criminals often target those who are alone because they are more vulnerable. Encouraging your child to walk home from school with a friend increases their safety and helps them build friendships. Teach them the importance of sticking with a buddy whenever they go out. You can start reinforcing this habit at home during every-day activities. For instance, suggest they bring a friend when they need to run an errand. This practice promotes essential habits that contribute to their safety.

Another tool to keep your family safe is establishing code words. A code word can be any word or short phrase that parents or guardians set up with their kids. This word ensures it is safe for them to go with another adult, like a relative, especially when they are unaware of the plans beforehand. This could be in cases where something unexpected comes up, or an emergency arises. If someone comes to pick them up and does not know the code word, they will know not to go. This simple step adds an extra layer of safety for situations that are out of the ordinary.

When most people hear the phrase "self-defense," they think of learning how to throw a punch or block a knife thrust. While these skills are undoubtedly important, they are not the first thing you should focus on. If you end up in a situation where you need to use physical skills (like punches and kicks) to defend yourself, then it means you have likely failed to be aware of the threat before it happens.

If you know what to look for, you can spot clues of a dangerous situation before they threaten you or your family. If you miss these early signs, you must react to the danger instead of proactively avoiding it. However, by investing just a few hours into learning the basics of situational awareness, you can gain a substantial advantage and avoid most potential threats.

For example, when you walk into a room, most people do not stop to observe the "baseline" situation. What is the general noise level? How are people supposed to be acting toward each other in this setting? What is the general mood of the room? What do you expect to find here, and so on? This only takes a few seconds of thought, but taking the time to assess the baseline of your area will give you a heads-up if things are about to take a turn for the worse.

Think of the last time you walked into a relaxed restaurant or your favorite coffee shop. As you walk in, the noise level is moderate, filled with the sounds of quiet conversations and the hiss of the espresso machine. Customers are scattered throughout the space, filling the air with a gentle buzz of productivity and relaxation. The clinking of coffee cups and occasional laughter contribute to the overall feeling of community. This is the baseline of the situation.

Imagine you have just placed your order and are sitting in a quiet corner, about to open your laptop and check some emails. Suddenly, two men start shouting at the bartender. This is not in line with the normal behavior you expected for this situation. While others in the coffee shop might be too focused on their work to notice or act like nothing threatening is happening, you already know this behavior is unusual for this setting. You should be ready to react quickly to a possible escalation.

Or, what if you walk into the coffee shop and can't see a single employee behind the counter? While that might not point to a threat, it is certainly out of the ordinary, and you should at least be alert to it. Anytime the baseline of a situation you are in changes, make yourself aware of it and assess if this change could indicate a potential threat to you or those around you. This will only take a second or two, but figuring this out ahead of time will enable you to react much sooner in a crisis.

In a world of uncertainties, learning self-defense and being aware of potential dangers is not just a choice but a necessity. Police may not always be nearby when needed, so we must equip ourselves and our families with the skills and awareness to handle potential threats. By teaching our children to stay alert, act confidently, and understand the value of their belongings, we give them the tools to deter attackers. Simple practices, like using the buddy system and setting up code words, can greatly enhance their safety. Situational awareness, in particular, is a vital skill that helps us recognize and react to dangers before they fully develop. These proactive steps empower us to protect our families and create additional security in an unpredictable world.

2

TRAINING UNDER FIRE

FBI Citizens Academy to CIA Recruitment

"Get down! Everyone, face down!" The man with tattoos covering his arm, wearing a black mask, turned sharply and locked eyes with me, sending a shiver down my spine. "I said down!" he shouted, his voice echoing through the room. My heart pounding, we quickly huddled on the cold, hard floor, the distant sounds of gunfire growing louder and more threatening with each passing second.

Time seemed to slow, each heartbeat pounding in my ears. The air was thick with fear and confusion; every muscle in my body was tense and ready to move. The silence was fragile, ready to break at any second.

Suddenly, the stillness shattered with a loud "Boom!" The door flew open and smashed against the wall as trained FBI agents, wearing tactical vests and heavily armed, stormed into the room with military precision. Their forceful entrance sent a shockwave through the room, making us cringe in response.

"Clear! Clear!" the agents shouted, their voices firm and confident. They moved efficiently, their eyes scanning every corner and shadow. The man with the tattooed arms was quickly disarmed and subdued, revealing him to be an undercover federal agent.

This intense scene occurred at an FBI training facility, where we volunteered to play hostages. Normally calm and organized, the compound became a battleground for this exercise. The tattooed man was not the threat he seemed to be but a vital part of this SWAT demonstration for the FBI Citizens Academy.

As part of the program, we were put into scenarios with active shooters and defensive tactics to give us a glimpse into the intense world of federal law enforcement. The experience was shocking, as the line between training and real fear blurred because of the realistic enactment.

Once we were safe, the agents helped us to our feet, their earlier intensity replaced by reassuring professionalism. Our adrenaline was still high, but we felt relieved as we processed what we had just been through. This was not just a drill; it was a powerful reminder of the dangers faced by those who protect us and the thin line between safety and chaos.

My friend Jim, an FBI sniper trainer, had introduced me to the course. He suggested I join an immersive program offering an insider's look at the agency. The special agent in charge selected me for their intensive eight-week program, which included classes on cybercrime, terrorism, white-collar crime, and human trafficking.

In one of the classes taught by a seasoned federal agent, the instructor looked around the room and asked, "Who here has a first aid kit in their car?" I raised my hand, eager to show my preparedness.

"And what do you have in your first aid kit?" he asked, his gaze intense.

"Band-Aids and Neosporin," I replied, trying to sound confident.

He stared at me and said, "If Band-Aids and Neosporin can solve your problem, then you do not have a problem."

The room went silent as he continued, explaining how many deaths from car accidents or battlefield injuries could be prevented with the right tools and quick action. His words hit hard as he taught us how to stop bleeding and open airways—skills that could mean the difference between life and death.

These lessons became essential to our skillset, preparing us for the dangerous years ahead as we worked undercover in the world's most dangerous environments.

Getting the proper training and tools to save a life will give you peace of mind, knowing you are doing everything possible to keep your family safe. As discussed earlier in the book, this is a way to expand your circle of influence to handle things that come into your circle of concern. In the chaotic moments after a severe injury, quick action can stop significant blood loss and ensure the person can breathe, stabilizing them until professional medical help arrives.

According to the National Institutes of Health, severe bleeding, or hemorrhage, is one of the leading causes of preventable death in trauma cases, making up about 40 percent of these deaths. With the proper training and tools like tourniquets and clotting gauze, bystanders can significantly reduce the risk of death from severe bleeding.

Tourniquets are especially effective in stopping heavy bleeding from limb injuries. When used correctly, a tourniquet can stop blood flow and prevent the patient from dying. The time it takes for emergency medical services to arrive can vary greatly, especially in rural or remote areas. In these critical minutes, a trained person can use a tourniquet on a victim, significantly improving their chances of survival. Research shows that using tourniquets before getting to the hospital has a success rate of over 90 percent in controlling severe limb bleeding.

Thanks to the thorough training in the FBI course, I became convinced of the importance of first-aid trauma response training and made it mandatory for our team members. Years later, that decision saved a teammate's life.

One of our men suffered a severe cut on his arm, a wound that would have caused fatal blood loss before reaching the hospital. But because his comrade acted quickly and used his recent training, a tourniquet was applied, and he survived. They had just taken the course taught by my friend and former Green Beret Jeff Kirkham, who invented the Rapid Application Tourniquet System (R.A.T.S), the fastest tourniquet on the market and proven in combat. In that critical moment, the quick reaction and life-saving skills from our training made all the difference. That day, a life was saved because we were prepared.

Another important part of emergency care is making sure someone can breathe. Airway blockage can happen for different reasons, such as the tongue blocking the throat in unconscious people or swelling from an injury. Nasal and oral airway kits are designed to keep the airway open so the victim can breathe. According to the National Safety Council, about 5,000 deaths each year in the US are due to airway obstruction. Immediate action with airway management tools can greatly reduce this number.

Having the proper training and tools during an accident is not just helpful; it can be essential for saving lives. The ability to stop blood loss with a tourniquet or clotting gauze and to ensure an open airway with nasal or oral airway kits can stabilize a victim until emergency medical help arrives. Knowing how to act quickly can mean the difference between life and death. These skills are vital when conducting undercover child rescue missions and for parents and caregivers to know in an emergency. This knowledge can significantly reduce preventable deaths and improve outcomes for trauma victims.

The FBI training continued for eight weeks, covering everything from fingerprint lifting to cybercrime. It was during these classes that I met some key people who would introduce me to the world of anti-child trafficking. One of them, who we will call Augustus, would later become a leading political figure in the fight against modern human slavery. Over the next few years, we trained together on everything from long-range sniper shooting to Krav Maga.

Beyond our passion for tactical training, Augustus and I shared a unique connection. We were each recognized as part of the "Forty under 40" elite—the forty most influential people under forty years old in our state. Augustus earned honors for his relentless fight for justice in law enforcement, while my recognition came from charitable contributions and the success of my investment fund. Our shared commitment to positively impacting children's lives and supporting law enforcement brought us together at numerous philanthropy fundraisers. We frequently served on charity boards and contributed in various ways.

Any project that benefited children was a top priority, so when a former Miss America requested help sponsoring an event for kids who had lost a parent in military service, the decision to support was made quickly. The event aimed to support young girls suffering from loss by crowning them onstage. With a friend, we helped cover expenses for flights, hairdressers, and hotels for the families. We were invited to attend the pageant and witness the beautiful experience of the children.

I called Augustus, who was pursuing an influential political career, playfully addressing him as A.G. "What is up, A.G.?" I greeted. "I have got front-row tickets to the Miss America pageant. It would be fun if you could join me."

Augustus responded swiftly, "Hutch, unlike you, I have a reputation to uphold. I can't be seen front row at the Miss America pageant with you."

I quickly clarified, "No, it is not like that. My friend and I are sponsoring young girls who lost their fathers in military battles this past year. We are covering their expenses for the pageant and allowing them to experience the joy of a former Miss America crowning them onstage. It is a beautiful charity event for the children."

His tone shifted, "Oh, that is super cool. I will go with you to that."

We flew to Atlantic City for the pageant and met families who had lost fathers and spouses that year. Understanding their difficult situation, we wanted to bring them joy and ease their pain, even for a moment. We made every effort to treat the little girls like true princesses, helping them feel the love and support of others during their darkest times.

While many view pageants as promoting the objectification of women or setting unrealistic beauty standards for young girls—an issue we will explore in later books—I want to acknowledge the fantastic people involved in this pageant who genuinely strive to contribute positively to the world. These women, not only intelligent and talented but also deeply compassionate, showed genuine care for the children who had lost their fathers. Seeing the smiles on the little girls' faces as a former Miss America crowned them was heartwarming.

Since it was a charity event for fallen soldiers, the Pentagon sent a representative. He was a former CIA recruiter with over two decades of experience identifying ideal candidates to assist the agency. After enjoying a few days at the pageant, we were at a dinner with Augustus, a few former Miss Americas, and the CIA recruiter.

Midway through dinner, the recruiter leaned forward and said, "Mr. Hutchinson, I have been observing you for the last three days, and I believe your country could benefit from your unique talents."

I chuckled and asked, "Well, what talents might those be?"

He responded, "I have identified people with skills like yours throughout my career. Your ability to break down communication barriers and form instant connections with a diverse range of people, from a homeless person to a billionaire and a runway model, is exceptional. You could excel in undercover investigations involving illicit financial activities."

He continued, "Imagine this: We fly you to Dubai, align you with people suspected of laundering money, and you become their confidant, extracting the needed information. Your background running a large investment fund provides the perfect cover."

When his people followed up a few weeks later, I declined the offer. Stepping into danger for white-collar criminals in Dubai didn't seem appealing. With our investment fund thriving and the philanthropic work fulfilling, life had become the realization of my long-held dreams. While I appreciate the task forces dedicated to combating such crimes, it didn't align with my goals at the time. Little did anyone know, another opportunity would present itself about a year later—one that couldn't be refused.

3

THE POWER OF GIVING

Be Charitable to Become successful

" **I** want to be rich!"

"Why?" my mentor asked, eyes seeing right through my ambitions.

"I want to travel the world, host extravagant parties, drive nice cars, fly a plane, own a helicopter, live in a beautiful house, and after all that, I want to help people."

"You have it all backward," this mentor replied. "If you begin your career by helping people, everything else will fall into place. Do you want to be a millionaire? Start by finding a way to create a million dollars worth of value in the lives of others. Do you want to be a billionaire? Decide you will provide humanity with a billion dollars worth of impact."

This conversation took place in my early 20s, during a time of confidence in future success, though the path to achieving it was unclear. However, the critical importance of having mentors was already evident. Just as hiring top self-defense trainers was essential for acquiring the skills needed for undercover work, finding a mentor or coach in business and life was equally vital. While experience is often said to be the best teacher, this proved only partially true. The experiences of others, particularly those who had already faced similar challenges, provided even better lessons. Learning from someone else's journey offered valuable insights that accelerated success in many areas.

One mentor gave me advice that completely transformed my financial pursuits and almost everything about my life. He taught me the importance of charity work. "Commit to donating money now, and you will find building your business becomes much smoother," he advised. "The average person allocates about 2 percent of their income to charity. If you decide to donate 15–20 percent today, you will witness a direct impact on your financial career, achieving financial freedom much faster."

I asked, "Wouldn't it be easier to wait until I am wealthy to give money away? Logically, if my current income is focused on reinvesting in the business instead of donating, there would be more money to give later. Wouldn't that help the business grow faster?"

My concern continued, "Also, 20 percent is a very high percentage. Right now, our family income is only $2,000 per month. Are you suggesting we live on $1,600 instead? Our family is already struggling, and we might have to work extra hours to pay the bills."

Ignoring my objections, my mentor responded, "Alongside donating money, I suggest spending up to 20 percent of your working time in philanthropy."

"My time, too?" I complained. "What about work-life balance? Now I have to juggle work, life, and charity?"

He assured me that actively pursuing a life of giving was a key component to success in all areas of life, including financial success. He explained that integrating charity into my routine would enrich my personal life and provide unique opportunities for growth and networking in my professional life.

At the time, this concept seemed illogical to me. *I wanted to be successful so I could be charitable, never considering that I should be charitable to become successful.*

Reflecting on my career, I am certain that the decision to contribute generously to making a difference in the lives of others greatly impacted the success of my companies and my satisfaction with life. It is important to decide to give back now; do not wait until you are successful to make a difference. You will observe a direct correlation between your choices to help others and the success in your worthwhile goals and dreams, including financial goals.

Whether you call it karma, the universal law of exchange, or blessings from God, it undeniably works. The book of Malachi in the Bible states that when we choose to help others, the windows of heaven will pour out blessings to the extent that there won't be enough room to receive them. I have experienced this divine abundance in my life because of my choice to be generous.

This advice from my mentor was a turning point in my understanding of wealth and success. The traditional view of becoming rich often revolves around personal gain, luxury, and status. But true, lasting wealth comes from a foundation of generosity and service to others. The most impactful and sustainable success stories are built on the principle of adding value to the lives of others.

Before you even begin creating wealth, find ways to be charitable and give in ways that truly impact the lives of others or benefit the world as a whole. This approach sets the stage for financial success and enriches your journey with purpose and fulfillment.

Charitable giving is not just a moral obligation but a powerful tool for creating lasting change. When you give, you create a ripple effect that extends far beyond the initial act of kindness. Whether you donate to a local shelter, fund educational programs, or support global programs, your contributions can transform lives and communities.

Remember that being philanthropic does not always mean giving money. Your time, skills, and resources are equally valuable. Volunteering at a nonprofit, mentoring someone in need, or using your talents to support a cause can have a powerful impact. It is about leveraging what you have to make a difference.

True wealth is not measured by the number of zeros in your bank account but by the positive impact you create. By starting with a mindset of giving and service, you lay a strong foundation for meaningful and rewarding success.

While driving through the city with a friend one afternoon, I spotted a man on the roadside holding a sign that read, "Homeless, anything helps." I pulled over and offered some cash, which the man gratefully accepted.

As I merged back into traffic and rolled up my window, my friend turned to me and asked, "Do you genuinely believe giving money to that guy is making a difference?"

"I do not know, and I can't judge," I responded. "Who is to say that guy could not have been me on the side of the road if I had not been fortunate to be born into a healthy home."

Regrettably, as I learned more about the issue of homelessness, it became evident that simply handing out cash might contribute to the problem by enabling a welfare mentality. What I believed to be genuine assistance was unintentionally perpetuating a condition that did not build self-esteem or give these individuals the skills needed to lift themselves out of their situation. It was a challenging realization, but I finally decided to focus most of my attention on charities supporting the cause of protecting the truly innocent: children.

I spent a few years working with Primary Children's Hospital, where I was deeply moved by the strength and determination of those kids recovering from life-threatening accidents or illnesses. Witnessing their resilience in such hardships was incredibly inspiring. I found great fulfillment in participating in charities that aimed to ease the pain of families facing such difficult situations.

My involvement in philanthropy went beyond just donating money and volunteering. I actively promoted fundraising events, working tirelessly to raise awareness and support for these important causes. I organized events, rallied community support, and raised considerable money to fund essential medical treatments and services for the children.

I also made it a personal mission to donate generously to many charities dedicated to improving the lives of these young patients. Every dollar raised and every effort made felt like a step toward easing the weight on these families and providing hope during their darkest times.

This work at Primary Children's Hospital and my involvement in related charitable activities reinforced my belief in the power of community and compassion. It showed me firsthand the powerful impact that collective efforts and generosity can have on the lives of those in need. The experience shaped my career path and deepened my commitment to making a difference for future generations.

I worked with many different foundations that brought hope and healing to children. For seven years, I was on the Utah board of directors for the Make-A-Wish Foundation, which grants life-changing wishes to children with critical illnesses. Helping to fulfill these wishes became one of the highlights of my humanitarian work. We made dreams come true for kids with cancer, like riding in a Lamborghini or going to Disneyland when their families could not afford it. Some wished to meet celebrities like Jackie Chan, and we made it happen.

Today, my shelves are filled with numerous awards, including the Ellis Island Medal of Honor, the International Medal of Freedom, honorary doctorate degrees, and even a medal from racing the Baja 1000. However, my most cherished prize is a simple star, representing the children of Make-A-Wish whose wishes were granted because of my efforts.

God's blessings for doing good, or what some may call the universal law of exchange, are real. Choose to make a positive impact in the world and the lives of others out of the pure generosity of your heart, and you will receive abundance in ways you never thought possible. This has proven true in my life many times.

Years after I started doing child rescue work, I received a call from one of the groups I supported. The coordinator told me about a major influencer who wanted to launch his anti-trafficking campaign in Bangkok, but it would cost over $100,000 to make it happen.

"One hundred thousand dollars!" I exclaimed, feeling a mix of shock and concern.

"Yes," the man responded, "That is the cost to get this influencer and his team to Thailand to film some of our efforts against child exploitation there." The foundation he was working with was pretty new, and that kind of money for a trip was not feasible.

"He has millions of followers, and this will make a huge impact in the fight against trafficking," he explained. "If you are willing to fund the trip, we could help millions of people get behind the mission of fighting for this cause."

My business partner, Don, had lived in Bangkok for many years and deeply loved the Thai people. Together, we funded the trip and accompanied the influencer's team to Thailand for a successful mission.

As we returned home and the plane touched down in the US, my phone regained signal. It started vibrating with missed calls and texts, and I began to listen to the voicemail messages.

"Hi Paul," I recognized the voice as one of the owners of the largest hotel chain in the world. "I have been reviewing your email and am interested in investing ten million dollars in your company."

"Wow!" I thought, feeling a surge of gratitude and disbelief. "That voicemail message felt like a gift from God."

Then, I listened to the next voicemail. "Hi Paul, this is Jon," the message continued. "I represent a firm you presented to a few weeks ago, and we are ready to invest with you." His offer was even higher than the first voicemail I received. My income from those two voicemails would far exceed what I had just spent on the charity trip to Thailand.

The experience was overwhelming. Divine grace rewarded my efforts to help others in ways I could never have predicted. I felt deeply grateful, knowing I was fighting on the winning team.

Engaging in charitable work has shown me that our actions can have far-reaching effects. Each act of kindness and generosity has a far-reaching impact, touching lives in ways we may never fully understand. The smiles on the children's faces when their wishes are granted, the relief in the eyes of their parents, and the feeling of community that comes from working together are all priceless rewards.

The connections and relationships built through these philanthropic activities often lead to unexpected blessings. Whether forming lifelong friendships, gaining new perspectives, or finding unexpected support during tough times, the benefits of giving go beyond what we can see or touch. They enrich our lives with experiences and memories that money can't buy.

True wealth is not measured by what we accumulate but by what we give. The joy of seeing a child's dream come true, the satisfaction of knowing you made a difference, and the love and gratitude you receive are invaluable. These treasures fill our hearts and lives, proving that the more we give, the richer we become.

4

AMASSING WEALTH AND CHANGING COURSE

Unveiling the Darkness of Child Trafficking

During my teenage years, posters of Lamborghini's and Ferrari's hung on my wall. One had a quote that read, "He who has the most toys wins."

As maturity brought the realization that money could be earned while making a positive impact on others' lives, a new personal motto was embraced: "The person who has a powerful, positive impact on the most lives wins."

Money is neither inherently good nor bad; it simply provides choices. It allows people to decide which car to buy or which neighborhood to live in. Some use money to fulfill their desires, while others use it to contribute to a better world.

It would be nice to say my pursuit of financial abundance was purely driven by the goodness of my heart, but philanthropy wasn't the only motivation. I had big dreams of providing a comfortable lifestyle for my family and myself. While there's nothing wrong with aspiring to a life of abundance, if the focus shifts away from helping others, all the wealth in the world becomes unfulfilling.

As my career progressed, my mantra became, "I will do today what the average person won't do so I can enjoy tomorrow what the average person can't even comprehend." My vision board showcased a lavish house with a home theater, a pool, fast cars, global travels, jets, yachts, and more—The intense drive for what was believed to be massive success eventually paid off. At twenty-nine, my first company was sold for over twenty million dollars, mostly in restricted stock of a public company. On paper, wealth was achieved, and at the time, I believed the image of wealth defined success.

For many years, hard work was a priority. Together with John, we co-founded an investment fund known as Bridge Loan Capital, which evolved into Bridge Investment Group. With thousands of employees and billions of dollars under management, we built a world-class team with global recognition. Hard work created a lifestyle for me and my business partners that most could only dream of, with luxurious homes, exclusive parties, and traveling the world on private jets. My relationships with celebrities, politicians, and professional athletes made me feel important. I was married to an NFL cheerleader, and my life symbolized my view of success at the time.

Then, in the summer of 2014, a phone call changed everything. It was Augustus, my good friend from the FBI training event years before. He said, "Paul, I would like to introduce you to someone. He has something important to share with you."

I replied, "Great! When can we meet?"

He answered, "I want to bring him to your movie night this evening."

My friend JP had sold his company for over a billion dollars and had built a beautiful theater in his home. A bunch of friends and fund investors were going to be there, enjoying a movie together. We had a rule: no pitches, just friends getting together to have fun.

So, I told Augustus, "No. We told the guys we would not have anybody coming to present anything. We are just getting together for a movie night at JP's."

He replied, "Paul, this one is different. This guy is a former Homeland Security agent, and he wants to share with us how he has identified about twenty children in Colombia who are being trafficked; he wants to rescue them. He wants to raise money for the rescue operation and help start his new foundation."

"Trafficked? What does that mean?" I asked.

"Sold, just like slaves at the time before the Civil War," he replied.

"Sold for what?" I responded.

"Sold for sex, organ harvesting, you name it…"

Helping children was the focal point of my charity work, and I could not imagine anything worse than a child being sold. This was the first time I had heard of something like this, and I was interested in hearing more.

Augustus explained how he and another of our mutual friends, Josh (the son of a former Presidential candidate), had met with some people who were creating an anti-child-trafficking organization. Throughout this book, I will refer to this organization as ACTO (not its real name).

A former Homeland Security agent, whom we will call Cassius, spearheaded the effort. The meeting discussion focused on strategies for gaining traction for the new group. They discussed securing wealthy donors, enlisting ambassadors for additional support, and identifying key players for the rescue missions.

The idea was to document undercover rescue missions and share these stories with the public. Cassius's vision involved enticing perpetrators to gather all their victims in one location for a staged party. This would provide him an opportunity to capture their stories on camera.

To execute this plan, he emphasized the need for someone capable of playing the role of a wealthy buyer. Part of the demand for such trafficking in developing countries often comes from wealthy people with financial resources and big egos, most of whom are from the United States.

In describing the key positions required for this team, Cassius highlighted how there was no shortage of special forces operators; they had plenty of those. They lacked a wealthy playboy with negotiation skills who could navigate dangerous situations. Recalling the earlier meeting with the former CIA recruiter, Augustus inquired if they had heard of Paul Hutchinson. Josh responded, "Oh, Paul would be perfect!"

Later, I humorously commented, "I am not sure that is a compliment! You both thought I would be a good undercover pedophile!" Over the years, they introduced me to various groups, emphasizing how I had a unique set of skills. As told to the recruiter years before, there was still uncertainty about what specific skills they were referring to. Still, the commitment remained strong to use whatever tools were available to combat child abuse and trafficking.

Part of the ACTO strategy involved having wealthy donors participate in the rescue missions, which exposed them firsthand to the harsh reality of trafficking. They believed such an experience would build a commitment to the cause that could not be achieved in any other way.

Augustus knew of my efforts to help raise millions of dollars for child-related charities, and this one seemed more important than any of them. I agreed to let him bring this man to the event.

At the end of our movie night, Augustus stood up and introduced Cassius. He told us of finding children in Colombia who were being sold as sex slaves and how many of the people engaged in this horrific activity were from the United States. He told us there were more people in slavery today than all three hundred years of the transatlantic slave trade put together.

I could not believe what I was hearing! Did slavery still exist? I was taught in school that slavery was abolished at the time of the Civil War. The worst part was how this guy was talking about *children*. How far removed from moral principles does someone have to be to harm innocence in this way?

As I absorbed the details of Cassius's story and imagined the pain of what those kids must be going through in Colombia, a knot formed in my stomach. I had seen families torn apart by losing a child to cancer. We had helped starving kids in Africa with flies on their faces. We had comforted families who lost a child to suicide, but this was a whole new level of pain and darkness.

What does this say about the human condition when slavery is still accepted in any form, let alone in the case of a child being sold for sex, organ harvesting, or even labor camps? My heart knew I would help fight this in any way possible. If my goal was to impact the lives of others positively, what would be more fulfilling than helping pull these kids out of Hell?

The room was filled with my friends and high-net-worth investors. Some doubted the validity of the numbers and suspected Cassius of having ulterior motives. Over the next few days, I received multiple texts from a few friends warning me about one of the men associated with ACTO facing fraud investigations.

I was eager to contribute to the fight against child trafficking. Close relationships with people who could write large checks were in my network, and I was willing to bring in their contributions and also address issues when something lacked integrity. A conversation with ACTO was initiated, urging them to clean up their image if they wanted to attract donors from my associates. Advice was given on the importance of having competent, trustworthy people on their team if they were to start a non-profit. I offered to introduce them to individuals who would donate millions, but it was clear they couldn't be involved with anyone facing fraud allegations.

Cassius asked me to help resolve the problem with his employee. This was the first of many times he asked me to "fix" a situation. He said anyone who would stand in the way of his mission needed to be dealt with if we wanted to help the children. I agreed to help protect those who were rescuing the kids. I met with the offender multiple times and discussed how being authentic was the only way to manage his financial problems. In the end, many people from the original group were found to lack integrity.

Every person on earth has faults. We are all imperfect in many ways. One lesson I learned from this fight against evil is how the internal battle is the most important. Most of us are imperfect people trying to get better every day. We all want to imagine a true hero without flaws, but no human can claim such a title. I have worked with hundreds of great men and women in this fight against child trafficking who had past addictions, broken marriages, financial challenges, and even legal battles. Some experienced childhood trauma themselves, which led to a life of sexual promiscuity. They had worked through their pain and were now using it to better themselves and bless the lives of others.

My own life at the time was far from perfect. My twenty-year marriage was heading for a divorce. I found unhealthy satisfaction in extravagant parties and spending money on fancy cars and clothes. Even though many people saw me as extremely successful, a failing marriage and the pursuit of material things left me unsatisfied.

I desperately sought fulfillment and meaning, and the opportunity to help free the children became transformative. For most of the undercover operators I worked with, fighting the evil of child abuse and trafficking brought us closer to God. It gave us purpose.

Over the years, I have worked with operators from almost every religion: Muslims, Christians, Jews, Hindus, and even Buddhists. These operators, who put their lives on the line for the safety of these innocent children, are true heroes.

Maintaining humility and a solid spiritual foundation was essential, especially when dealing with such a sensitive subject. Unfortunately, some people let the darkness of trafficking drain their energy and weaken their moral principles. It became painfully clear that this battle was not just against flesh and blood but against a deep darkness and wickedness that had infiltrated human existence. The abuse of a child's innocence comes from evil forces that are widespread in our world. It takes great spiritual strength and unwavering conviction to survive the darkness that comes with this work.

This is not a political or religious issue but a fight to save humanity from an evil beyond comprehension. As my team stood on the front lines of this battle, we realized that our efforts were more than rescue missions—they were a desperate plea for light in a world overshadowed by unbelievable darkness. Each child's life we saved was a ray of hope, proof of the infinite power of good in the face of overwhelming evil. This fight, this mission, was about preserving the very essence of humanity, and it demanded everything we had and more.

Part II

The Island

The Cartegena Colombia Rescue Mission

5

FROM OPULENCE TO VULNERABILITY

The Beginning of a Dangerous Mission

"Can you be in Colombia in two days?" The voice on the other side of the phone sent a jolt through me, a blend of danger and excitement. This call would change my life forever.

It was the morning of September 18th, 2014, and I was in Atlanta, Georgia, with my business partner, Don. We were attending an exclusive conference with multi-generational billionaire families and staying in an opulent hotel that shielded us from the world's harsh realities. Our success had propelled us into a realm of financial security and gained respect from the most affluent families on the planet.

Our purpose at the conference was to raise money for our investment fund, showcasing how our real estate model could enhance wealth and preserve generational security for the attendees. Although Don had spent holidays assisting orphanages in third-world countries, and I had been actively involved in charity boards aiding suffering children, we were, in essence, sheltered from the inconceivable hardships faced by many beyond our privileged bubble. Little did I know that my understanding of the world was on the verge of a transformative shift.

Amid the luxurious setting of the hotel, I received a call from Cassius. His voice was urgent and filled with concern. "Paul, I am in Cartagena, Colombia. Remember our suspicion about over twenty children being trafficked in the area? We now have intel suggesting over fifty children are being sold by related rings in Cartagena and more than a hundred victims in other cities. We need simultaneous sting operations in three cities to rescue them all."

I assumed he needed additional funding for the rescue mission and asked, "How much money do you need for a successful operation?" Instead, he said, "No, I need *you*. Can you be in Colombia in two days?" My heart raced; I had heard stories of Colombia's dangers, but the prospect of participating in a genuine rescue mission transcended any fears. My charitable efforts had always extended beyond monetary contributions, and physically aiding those children in need resonated deeply with me.

As the weight of his words sank in, I realized this was a pivotal moment. The comfort and security of my current life stood in stark contrast to the unimaginable suffering of those victims. The urgency of the situation demanded immediate action, and I knew that my response to this call would shape not only the lives of those children but also the course of my own life.

Details of the operation unfolded: a sex tourism hotel project, trafficked children sold under the guise of a fake modeling agency, and the urgent need to gather them in one location for a simultaneous rescue. The plan involved me posing as a wealthy investor, expressing interest in funding their project, provided they could prove to me that they had the children already in their possession.

While logic shouted the obvious dangers of going undercover in Colombia as a wealthy businessman from the US, a strange calmness comforted me. Fueled by the belief that we were confronting the ultimate evil and protected by God and all the virtuous forces of the universe, I immediately agreed to join the mission.

My business partner, Don, witnessed my swift acceptance and must have passed the information on to my co-founder, John. Within an hour, John called me, questioning the wisdom of my decision.

"Have you thought this through?" He reasoned, "Going to Colombia as a wealthy buyer to lure in child traffickers is incredibly dangerous!"

John continued, "Your company is flourishing. You could work a few more years, retire, buy an island, and live happily the rest of your life."

"Would I truly be happy?" I countered, "If I bought an island, a yacht, or a private jet, would any of that bring me genuine happiness?"

I continued, "If you just learned that I was doing something else risky this week, like climbing Everest, we would be having the same conversation."

John answered, "Yeah, we probably would."

I concluded, "When I am ninety-five years old, talking to my great-grandchildren about my accomplishments, which would really matter? Climbing a mountain, building a billion-dollar company, or rescuing children from slavery?"

"If my profile, connections, background, or skillsets can help these poor victims, even if we only rescue one or two of them, it would be worth it."

He agreed, "Yeah, you are right, Paul. You are perfect for this role, and it is worth the risk to rescue those kids." Since then, John and Don have become staunch supporters, funding missions and participating in awareness efforts.

Once I committed to the mission, the undercover team sprang into action. They began showing the traffickers my existing online profile, presenting me as a wealthy investor interested in their sex resort venture. The perpetrators took the bait, and negotiations were arranged for a face-to-face meeting at a secluded restaurant on the beach. The traffickers now knew my name and were expecting my arrival later that week, adding a heavy layer of tension to an already dangerous situation.

The rest of the day, as I continued my usual job of raising real estate investment funds, the luxuries that once seemed so important—fancy hotels, expensive cars, extravagant dinners—did not matter anymore. My mind was consumed by the upcoming operation.

Could their plan to rescue the children really work? What safeguards would be in place to ensure our safety? Would I see my family again afterward? These questions kept swirling in my mind, each one more urgent than the last.

Every moment was filled with anticipation and determination. The seriousness of the operation weighed on me, making it hard to focus on anything else. My thoughts were all about the mission's details and necessities, from the planned logistics to the fact that I was the only one on the operation using my real identity. The stakes had never been higher, and the intensity of the commitment grew with each passing hour.

As a wealthy businessman interested in funding a resort project for the traffickers, my role required me to look the part. Fortunately, I already had everything needed to personify a potential investor. I was asked to arrive in Colombia within two days, dressed as a wealthy playboy, ready to negotiate a multi-million-dollar deal.

At the time of the phone call, I was wearing a handmade business suit that cost more than my first car. It was conservative blue on the outside and bold, bright pink on the inside. My custom shirt had monogrammed sleeves and diamond-studded cufflinks. I completed my look the following day with a Breitling Bentley watch and 18K gold aviator Ray-Ban sunglasses. I packed my Gucci bag and headed to the airport, ready to step into my role.

After many years of undercover work, my outfit now includes everything from a bulletproof business suit to handcuff keys embedded in my titanium paracord shoelaces. However, this first rescue mission was too short of notice to prepare the additional safety precautions. Fortunately, I had the outfit necessary to play the part of a wealthy potential business partner. And I had spent a lifetime acquiring the skills to keep me somewhat safe in a dangerous place.

The carefully planned rescue mission hit an unexpected problem. Two former Navy SEALs were supposed to pick me up in Cartagena to ensure my safety. However, a layover in Bogotá, Colombia, caused delays. Because of these delays, my plane missed the landing window in Cartagena, and I had to stay overnight in Bogotá.

The passengers were unhappy about the flight's cancellation, and tensions rose at the airport, almost leading to a riot. The atmosphere was thick with frustration and unease. I decided it was best to leave and find a place to stay for the night before continuing to Cartagena.

I knew the risks of being in a foreign country, especially dressed in expensive clothes, which made me stand out and look vulnerable. Despite this awareness, I had no choice but to leave the airport alone; my senses heightened, stepping into the unknown.

Walking out of the airport, a terrifying realization struck me: there was a time when gangs in Colombia could have someone killed for just two hundred dollars. The thought of my appearance in a place where a life could be worth so little made my pulse race. My flashy outfit and obvious signs of wealth painted a target on my back. Each step made me more aware of how foolish it was to arrive alone, dressed so extravagantly.

I exited the terminal and hailed what seemed like a reputable taxi. "Take me to the Marriott," I instructed. A while later, we passed a Marriott just off the freeway. My nerves felt uneasy as the driver continued past multiple exits.

My Spanish was quite limited. So, I said, "Ah, hola, Marriott right there!" He answered, "Hotel, hotel, hotel, and pointed ahead."

Alone in the back of the taxi, a knot of anxiety tightened in my stomach as the driver veered off the freeway and into a dark, seedy part of town. The streets were lined with gang members, drug dealers, and an intimidating group of large street thugs standing in the shadows. My heart pounded as the driver pulled over in front of a dimly lit motel that reeked of desperation and danger, a place where it seemed rooms could be rented by the hour. With a cold, detached nod towards the window, he said, "Hotel!"

While doing undercover work, it became absolutely clear that when intuition speaks, you listen. This was more than a gut instinct—my entire body screamed not to leave the taxi. It felt like a setup, and the sense of danger was overwhelming. With no weapons and the possibility of being severely outnumbered if things turned ugly, the risk was too great. In broken Spanish, I insisted, "No esta mi hotel! Necesito Marriott!"

"No!" he insisted, pointing at the rundown hotel. The argument went back and forth, but it became clear he wouldn't move until I left the taxi. What now? Getting out of the car seemed extremely dangerous, especially given how I was dressed. My internal guidance was clear: "Do not leave this car!"

Fumbling through my bag, a police badge given to me as an honorary colonel was found—a gift that may have saved my life that day. Pulling it out, I showed it to him and, in a firm voice, said, "Policia, Marriott, ahora!"

The driver, finally yielding to the intensity of my determination, reluctantly turned back to the Marriott. As we pulled into the hotel's secured area, the sight of armed guards holding assault rifles immediately caught my attention, a warning of the dangerous environment I was in. If I had exited the taxi in the other part of town, being robbed or even killed would have been almost certain.

The level of security was overwhelming, driving home the seriousness of the situation. Stepping out of the car, the weight of the decision to go undercover began to sink in. Each armed guard, each locked door, and each cautious glance made the reality of the threat unmistakably clear. This was not just another business trip but a dive into a world of danger where every moment could mean the difference between life and death. The mission ahead was dangerous yet critically important, and there was no turning back.

6

MEETING WITH TRAFFICKERS

Unmasking the Face of Evil

A loud applause erupted from the passengers as the plane landed in Cartegena. The undercover team was informed of my delay, causing a change in our carefully laid plans. Initially, I was supposed to fly into Cartagena the previous evening with enough time to prepare and hold a pre-operation meeting. However, with the unexpected delay, that plan went out the window. Instead, we would have to dive straight into action upon arrival, leaving no room for the preparatory steps meant to ensure everything ran smoothly.

This new reality meant showing up directly at the Cartegena airport, fully dressed in my expensive outfit that would, again, make me look like an appealing target. The need for immediate readiness added extra tension to the operation. To minimize risks, I arranged for secure transport from my hotel to the Bogota airport, bypassing any unnecessary exposure. The stakes were higher now, and every move needed to be executed with precision to ensure my safety and the mission's success.

Upon arriving at Cartagena airport, I was picked up by the two former special forces operators who served as my bodyguards. It made sense for the suspects to assume that someone of my income would have personal security. The traffickers were told I was an investor with a lot of money, ready to fund their operation. We were chauffeured by an undercover Colombian special agent in an unmarked, bulletproof SUV.

One of my companies manufactured bulletproof vests and armored vehicles, so I was very familiar with the various levels of ballistic protection. This knowledge gave me a detailed awareness of what each level could withstand. As I stepped into the vehicle they provided for my transport, I immediately assessed it as a Level B7. This meant the vehicle could endure heavy machine gun fire and armor-piercing rounds from super high-velocity rifles—basically a fortress on wheels, my kind of ride!

Initially, I felt relieved and secure in knowing we were well protected. But as we started our drive toward the traffickers, my relief transformed into a flood of questions. If such intense protection was necessary, what kind of weapons did the traffickers possess? My mind raced with a mix of unease and excitement, filled with images of heavily armed criminals and the potential confrontations that might await us.

The risk of the mission became increasingly apparent. If it were not for the children involved, I would never have willingly put myself in such danger. The operation held the promise of rescuing over one hundred victims and reuniting them with their families, which was the only justification for the risks involved. Despite the dangers I had already faced since arriving in Colombia, I believed that divine protection surrounded us because of the importance of our mission. The impact of this operation would extend far beyond my initial understanding, touching countless lives.

Reflecting on it, I realized my business partner, John, was probably right when he said, "Going to Colombia as a wealthy buyer to lure in child traffickers is really dangerous!" The danger was greater than I initially thought. Cassius and his team had used my real identity to gain credibility with the traffickers. And as part of the plan, they disclosed to the criminals that I was wealthy.

As I thought about the potential ways the criminals could profit from my presence, an unsettling question came to mind: Would the traffickers see me as more valuable for a ransom if they kidnapped me, or would they, instead, see my worth as a potential business partner? If they suspected even for a moment that this was a setup, what kind of resources would they arrange to capture me, knowing my real identity?

All kinds of possible situations ran through my mind. I hoped they would be convinced my presence could bring tens of millions of dollars into their business. I prayed they wouldn't jeopardize such a significant investment opportunity by disrupting the plan. Every detail of the operation had to be flawless, leaving no room for doubt or suspicion in the minds of these dangerous criminals.

The undercover Colombian agent, skillfully maneuvering our bulletproof car, took an exit leading us toward the beach. We parked directly on the sand, strategically positioned between the restaurant and the ocean. From this vantage point, both our team and the traffickers seated on the second-story balcony had a clear view of us.

Joseph, the top global Krav Maga trainer, was responsible for security for this operation. His unmatched skills and intense training ensured our team was ready for anything. Joseph, looking unassuming, could blend in without the traffickers knowing the incredible strength and skill that our security team possessed. They seemed completely unaware of the level of protection we had in place.

As the traffickers interacted with the undercover team, our bulletproof vehicle drove into view. The sight of this robust and armored car made a powerful statement, showing that I had the resources to fund their project. It subtly but effectively communicated the seriousness and support behind our mission, making our position even stronger in their eyes.

The ex-Navy SEALs got out of the vehicle and told me to stay inside as they walked around the perimeter to ensure an ambush was not set up. They opened my door, and I stepped out to be escorted by my security team into the restaurant. By design, the suspects could see us pull in and observe my bodyguards bringing me inside. This added to the credibility of my profile as an ultra-wealthy investor.

Heart pounding, I wondered what the next hour would bring. To my knowledge, I had never met a child trafficker before. Would they look like hardened criminals? Middle-aged, intimidating gang members with facial tattoos and multiple nose piercings came to mind. But nothing that day matched those expectations.

The suspects were young, energetic, clean-cut, and appeared more like business professionals than gang members. That experience taught a valuable lesson: never judge a book by its cover. Some of the kindest people have tattoos and body piercings, while some of the most deceitful criminals are well-groomed and use their religion as a reason to be trusted.

The traffickers were already captivated by the images of my extravagant lifestyle. We walked into the room and immediately saw the excitement on their faces. They were told I could fund their project and help turn their dreams into reality. Now, they were seeing their potential partner in real life, in the flesh. My clothes, my speech, and even my attitude were exactly what they expected from a wealthy Playboy investor. We had everything needed to lure them into bringing all their trafficked victims to our party so we could rescue them.

There were four suspects: three males and one female. Samuel was in his mid-twenties and very metrosexual. Fuego looked like a hustler who would do anything for money. Eduar was older, maybe in his early thirties, and carried himself like a businessman in charge of the operation.

The female appeared to be in her early twenties but had an arrogant attitude that rivaled Eduar. She was a young former beauty queen who we refer to as Linda Cerda. (Not her real name) She was beautiful on the outside, but this concealed her cold-heartedness on the inside. Her evil intent became apparent during the conversations over the next couple of hours. Handshakes with the men and a hug followed by a kiss on Linda's cheek were gestures designed to reinforce our carefully built credibility.

Seated in the restaurant, I positioned myself beside the undercover team while the traffickers sat across the table. As the conversation progressed and their despicable plans unfolded, the darkness of their intentions became even more apparent. Eduar revealed his plan to turn an inherited property into a child brothel resort, believing it would attract American clients. The chilling reality of their beliefs in profiting from the exploitation of children was sickening. Every word they said was incriminating, making their cruel intentions absolutely clear. With each passing moment, my urgency to stop them grew stronger.

Contemplating the situation, I asked myself, who is really to blame here? There was no doubt that anyone selling children needed to go to prison. Still, the fact that there was a market demand primarily driven by foreigners added another upsetting layer to the problem. Who were these buyers fueling the demand for such horrible acts? How could we stop the demand that kept this vicious cycle going? The solution was not just about catching traffickers; it was also about addressing the deeper issue of why such a market existed in the first place. Stopping the buyers was just as important as catching the sellers.

Samuel and Linda continued to explain their business and how they prey on the dreams of young innocents by luring them into their modeling company. Linda's credibility as a professional model and former beauty pageant contestant allowed her to lure children away from their families on the promise of fame and fortune. She would then sell them into the sex trade.

It felt even more alarming hearing these stories from a woman. We thought she would have demonstrated more compassion than the men, but her heart was filled with greed, and she had no compassion for the children's pain.

Fuego, the organizer of trafficking activities, was pure evil, obtaining an evil pleasure from causing pain to the vulnerable. Later, on the day of the party, he gave cocaine to an eleven-year-old boy who was being trafficked for the first time and was terrified it was going to hurt.

I could not help but think about the twisted paths that led these people into such darkness. Had they themselves been victims of abuse or bullying in their youth? Did a series of choices driven by anger, greed, and desperation set them on this destructive course? Perhaps they were influenced by environments of violence and neglect in their childhood, where cruelty became a means of survival. Regardless of their past, their complete lack of compassion for the innocence they destroyed was beyond my understanding. It was disturbing to realize that somewhere along the way, they had completely lost their humanity, becoming predators who thrived on the suffering of others.

If childhood trauma played a role in shaping these traffickers, then God bless the billions of people who have gone through similar pain but have chosen a different path. These good people used their suffering as a reason to protect innocence, making sure that the children in their lives never experience the horrors they went through. It shows the strength of the human spirit that so many people can turn their pain into compassion and a desire to protect others.

We all have a choice in how we handle our pain. The people sitting next to me at this meeting had chosen the darkest path, causing horrific suffering to their victims. Instead of breaking the cycle of abuse, they continued it, becoming the very monsters they might have once feared. The difference between those who use their pain to heal and those who use it to harm is distinct. This made our mission to stop them even more urgent and vital.

These people had lost their moral compass, leading them into unimaginable darkness. We have all seen hints of this behavior in those with inflated egos and low self-esteem. It often begins with disregarding others' feelings, gradually escalating into actions that inflict deep pain on those around them. People are on a dark and dangerous path when they view others as tools for their gain. This way of thinking removes compassion and humanity, leading to harmful and cruel actions.

Over the years of doing undercover missions, every trafficker we met had the same arrogant attitude, ignoring the value of life and virtue. Driven by greed and selfish desires, they exploited their victims for personal gain. I had seen the terrible effects of greed, arrogance, envy, and hatred before, but had never encountered anything this dark.

These traffickers did not just hurt people; they destroyed lives without a second thought. Their lack of empathy and complete disregard for the suffering they caused were shocking. Each encounter with them revealed just how far people could sink when they let greed and selfishness take over. This darkness was unlike anything we had ever seen, making our mission to rescue their victims even more critical.

Our intel informed us that this group, along with others in their network, was trafficking at least fifty children. We needed to convince them to bring every victim under their control to a party we would host in the next three weeks. Their evil business was built on greed and lust, which created the demand for their abuse. Now, we would use that same greed to bring them down.

The traffickers projected massive profits with the successful creation of their sex resort, believing that my involvement would help make it all happen. This belief would motivate them to bring all their existing victims to our sting operation. They were eager to show us their "assets" to secure my investment, unaware they were falling into a trap.

We had to make my partnership in their project seem irresistibly profitable, playing on their desires for wealth and power. Every detail had to be perfect to maintain the illusion. This was our chance to rescue the victims and take down the network. The traffickers' greed, which had driven their cruel enterprise, would now be the very thing that led to their downfall.

My role was to convince the traffickers I had the interest and capability to fund their resort. However, they had to prove they indeed had the children to make it successful. The undercover team, on the ground for weeks, had set up the operation and verified the number of victims being sold. Now, we had to convince them to bring every child to the same place at the same time.

Acting as an interested investor, I inquired about their plans for the resort. How much money was needed for construction? What was the planned location and project size? How many children were actively available, and what profit did they hope for?

Their detailed plan sickened me. They believed wealthy Americans would pay a substantial membership fee and additional charges for services. Through their trafficking network, they confirmed they could immediately provide more than fifty children for this resort. They sought millions of dollars from me to bring their vision to life, expecting tens of millions in annual profits once the project was completed.

7

I HAVE A GIFT FOR YOU

Rage Fueled by Compassion -
The Picture of an Innocent Child

As we discussed the traffickers' plans, they had no idea that we were collecting evidence against them. They did not suspect the black backpack in the corner had a hidden camera recording everything we said. Even the sunglasses one of our team members wore had a recording device.

Over the years in undercover work, I have been amazed by the creative ways cameras are hidden. We've used watches, hats, pens, room fans, radios, and even water bottles with tiny audio and video recorders inside. These clever devices help us gather the proof we need to catch the criminals without them knowing they are being recorded.

The traffickers continued talking with us, completely unaware of our plans to destroy their network. To anyone watching, we looked like ordinary people having a casual business lunch—a group of seemingly wealthy Americans making deals with Colombian businesspeople. But the true nature of our negotiations would be unimaginable to kind-hearted people.

Our conversations paused briefly as waiters served shrimp and pasta, then continued once they left. One of the other operators talked with the former beauty queen. At the same time, I kept discussing plans with Eduar, the greedy businessman, and Fuego, the ruthless trafficker who arranged transactions between buyers and sellers of the victims.

Expressing my interest in partnering with them and funding their project, I shared with them my primary concern: Ensuring they possessed sufficient "inventory" to justify my investment in the business. With their control of more than fifty victims already confirmed, we insisted on their commitment to bringing all the children to a single location so we could validate their possession of the young models essential for project success. To achieve this verification, we proposed hosting a party to be attended by some of my wealthy friends. If they could bring all the young models currently available for sale, and my friends find the event enjoyable, only then would I consider partnering with them on the development of their proposed sex resort venture.

As the traffickers determined my interest in funding their new venture, their enthusiasm increased. They were convinced their goal of establishing an illegal brothel catering to wealthy Americans was on the verge of realization. Fuego could not contain his excitement about our new partnership. Leaning eagerly across the table, he declared, "Pablo, I have a gift for you!"

I said, "Really? What is your gift?" He handed me his phone, which displayed a picture of an eleven-year-old girl. He said, "This is Princess. She is still a virgin. We just took delivery of some virgins. I am bringing her to the party just for you." Then he started to describe extremely graphic, horrific things we could do to this girl. My stomach was in knots. I wanted to vomit, but I needed to hold my composure.

I recognized this opportunity to help these new victims before anyone could ever hurt them. I thought to myself, "*If we could rescue the children before they were ever traumatized in the first place, it would be a miracle!*"

In the film *Sound of Freedom*, this girl was the main focus. The traffickers just called her "Princess." In the movie, Jim Caviezel handed a picture of the little girl to my character's driver. Looking at that child's face influenced my decision to join the rescue mission. In real life, however, I was already there, in Colombia, sitting next to some of the most heartless people on the planet.

But it was precisely at this moment when the trafficker showed me her picture on his phone that my commitment to the mission became unbreakable. Seeing her face made me more determined to protect the innocent and rescue these victims. This moment solidified my resolve to fight against such evil and do everything possible to save them.

I was ready to provide any resources needed to rescue this little girl. Thinking about my own experiences, especially having four younger sisters, made this mission even more personal. I remembered their innocence, excitement for life, and dreams for a bright future when they were her age. The idea that this girl had been captured by these heartless people and the horrors she would face was unimaginable to me.

The thought of what she must be going through fueled my determination. I could not stand the idea of someone so young and full of potential trapped in such a terrible situation. We had to do everything we could to save her and give her the chance to have the future she deserved.

The Navy SEAL positioned directly behind me said, "I am going to walk around the restaurant to make sure everything's all right." Later, during the debriefing, he told the team, "That little girl looked just like my daughter. I almost unholstered my weapon and shot him right there." He continued, "But, of course, if I took action, I would have jeopardized our cover, and we would have lost all the other children."

My fury intensified as Fuego shared the picture of this innocent little girl. It marked the first instance I saw a photograph of one of the victims, and suddenly, the harsh reality hit me. This was not a story told by one of the operators; it was happening right before my eyes. *It is inconceivable such cruelties truly occur.* Child trafficking is a horrible reality, more common than most people understand, and we were witnessing it firsthand in the most horrific manner. This trafficker was offering the innocence of this eleven-year-old child!

My feelings fluctuated from sorrow and anger to complete disgust. However, love was the powerful, sustaining emotion that carried me through this experience. It was a reflection of the infinite love God must have for these suffering victims. The love I felt for my sisters naturally extended to my compassion for this little girl, a child I had never met.

At that moment, I experienced calmness, an inner certainty that we could be the force for good and rescue her before she was harmed. My determination was fueled by the conviction that we could save her from this nightmare with our combined efforts and unwavering determination. The depth of my love and compassion gave me the strength to believe in our mission and the hope that we could bring light into her dark world.

Something the trafficker said made me realize he possessed more kids like her. I asked this trafficker if he had more virgins, knowing we needed to ensure their freedom before they were ever sold. He answered, "Oh yeah, I got three or four more."

I said, "You have to bring the virgins to the party for sure."

"No, they are too expensive!" he countered.

"What do you mean they are too expensive?" I asked, remembering that we had already committed to paying him $25,000 for this party: $500 per child for a minimum of fifty children for just two hours in the afternoon with them.

He responded, "Jefe (which means boss in Spanish), you are already paying $25,000. If you want to F### the other virgins, it is going to cost you an extra $2,000, maybe even more for that little one. It could cost you an additional $10,000."

At this point, I was legitimately pissed. No acting required! he was talking about these children as if they were commodities! My emotions, already simmering at the surface, erupted in a way that actually assisted the mission. In my well-tailored shirt and expensive Breitling watch, I placed my hands on my chest and proudly declared, "You do not think I can afford an extra ten thousand dollars?"

Fuego swiftly responded, "No, jefe, ¡no!"

I told him I wanted *every one* of those children brought to the party, especially the newly acquired virgins. I expressed my willingness to pay an additional amount if they could ensure the presence of every child they currently had. Then, with sternness, I emphasized, "They better still be virgins when they get there, or the deal is off. Do not touch them! They are reserved for me and my friends, *comprende?*"

He responded with a stupid grin, "Oh yeah, jefe, I understand!"

Then, Linda, the young beauty queen, raised objections to bringing the virgins. Given her limited English and my inadequate proficiency in Spanish at the time, one of our operators translated her conversation. We found ourselves intrigued by her resistance. Could it be she had more compassion than the male traffickers? We wondered why she would object, given our willingness to offer a substantial extra payment for the virgins.

However, her objections unveiled her true nature, revealing a level of depravity worse than some of the male traffickers. When asked about her discomfort with bringing the virgins, she explained they were not yet prepared. She further explained how she needed time to expose them to pornography and live sex acts to desensitize them.

Puzzled, I inquired, "What does that mean?" Her response implied that the victims needed to be *desensitized* to numb their emotions to prevent them from crying during the ordeal. She told us of their practice of giving drugs to make the kids more compliant, acknowledging that even with this, the virgins might cry if she could not adequately deaden their emotions in time. Shockingly, she concluded, "But if you are fine with them crying, then I am fine with them coming." The cruel reality of the situation these children were in weighed heavily on my heart, emphasizing the harsh truth of the evil unfolding before us.

It became evident that Linda's objections were empty of any compassionate concern. Instead, she was worried about the potential disapproval we might express if the victims cried while they were being raped. God help humanity; this was really happening to our children!

Sitting there, I felt overwhelmed by disgust. The evil at that table was unbelievable, hidden behind the faces of seemingly ordinary people. Despite their normal appearance, their actions and words revealed how wicked they were. I could not help but wrestle with a disturbing question: How far will arrogance, greed, and lust go to ruin the lives of others? How can humanity recover from such intense evil, opposite everything good?

As we finished the meeting, we secured commitments from the traffickers to bring their entire existing inventory of young models to the party for my friends and me. Although it meant enduring a few more days of torment for those victims, our team required this time to arrange the details for the sting operation's success. With their acknowledgment that they held over fifty victims in their network, our clear objective was to ensure every one of them was present at the party for their secure rescue.

Nearly a decade after that pivotal encounter with the traffickers, I revisited the same restaurant with my wife. As we walked to the exact table where that life-altering meeting took place, the emotions of that fateful day flowed within me. Sitting there with her, I relived the entire experience, reflecting on how it forever changed my life.

I thought about the countless children rescued by our teams over the years. My overwhelming gratitude for being part of such vital missions was indescribable. During the undercover operations, I had to keep my emotions in check, but returning to this place brought all those feelings rushing back.

I held my wife's hand, feeling deep gratitude for my life of purpose and fulfillment. The memories of those dark days were now surpassed with the hope and joy of knowing we had made a difference. Revisiting the venue became one of my life's most emotionally charged experiences, a powerful reminder of why we fight against such evil and the global impact of our efforts.

8

YOU ARE RIGHT,
GOD DID SEND ME!

A Mission of Divine Intervention and Moral Clarity

That first meeting with the suspects occurred three weeks before the planned rescue mission. Upon returning to the United States, my focus shifted entirely toward preparing for an operation that promised to transform my entire existence.

Back at home, surrounded by the comforts of a luxurious lifestyle, everything felt different. Living in a bubble had shielded me from the terrible pain and suffering that existed in the world. Hugging my kids tightly, it became clear how fragile and precious their safety truly was. Driving the new Tesla to work, my mind kept drifting back to the horrors witnessed and the innocent lives caught in the crossfire.

Thoughts of what would be done if one of my children were in that situation filled me with fierce determination. The mere idea stirred a resolve to give every penny to destroy the lives of anyone who dared to harm them. There was nothing our team wouldn't do to protect them, even if it meant putting our lives in danger.

This newfound awareness changed my perspective on life. The comfort and wealth that once defined my existence now seemed small compared to the mission of safeguarding innocence. My experiences had ignited a fire within me, a commitment to fight against the evil that preys on the vulnerable. As I navigated my daily life, I carried this resolve with me, determined to make a difference and ensure that no parent would ever have to face the nightmare of losing their child to such darkness.

Each day of those three weeks was a rollercoaster of intense emotions. As I carefully prepared for the mission, I was constantly overwhelmed by the knowledge of God's love surrounding the vulnerable victims in this terrible situation. This powerful feeling often brought me to my knees in prayer, seeking strength and guidance.

Realizing I had been chosen to help with this important mission made me feel deeply humbled. I felt a strong sense of responsibility, knowing that what we did could make the difference between life and death, freedom and continued suffering for these innocent children. My prayers became more intense, filled with gratitude and hope, asking for the wisdom and courage to face the dangerous path ahead.

Every moment had a purpose. I felt the mission's importance weighing on me, yet simultaneously, I experienced an incredible flood of empowerment. It was like I was being guided by an unseen hand, driven by a greater force than myself. This divine connection gave me the strength to push through the uncertainty and stay focused and determined.

As the days passed, my determination grew stronger. I knew that every sacrifice, every penny we would spend on this mission, was worth it if it meant saving even one child from these traffickers. The mission had become more than just a duty; it was a sacred calling. In those quiet moments of reflection, I felt an unshakable faith that we would succeed and bring light to the darkness and hope to the hopeless.

Since I had to go on the mission as Paul Hutchinson without the protection of a fake profile, my foresight and instinct for self-preservation led me to secure a burner phone with an undercover number before the operation began. This burner phone and a second WhatsApp account became indispensable tools in gaining Eduar's trust and ensuring he would bring all the children.

Over the next few weeks, I maintained a discreet line of communication with Eduar, using the burner phone to verify that he was successfully mobilizing his network of traffickers. This continuous contact was crucial in keeping him engaged and convinced of my legitimacy. Each message and interaction was carefully planned to avoid raising suspicion while pushing him toward our goal. To this day, I still have screenshots of those texts, preserving a detailed record of our interactions.

Eduar's increasing level of comfort in our communication reached a point where he willingly shared images of himself alongside the victims he was shamelessly exploiting. His classy shirts and his impeccably groomed appearance contradicted the dark reality of his involvement in this evil enterprise.

He drove around in a nice car and lived in what appeared to be a respectable neighborhood, creating a stark contrast between his public image and the world of child trafficking in which he operated.

Our text exchanges included the specifics of his plans for a sex hotel and the victims under his control. Within one of these disturbing conversations, Eduar unexpectedly forwarded a photograph of himself in his car, a broad smile illuminating his face, with his three-year-old daughter innocently seated in the back. The picture showed a surprising and confusing contradiction. It contrasted the warmth and happiness of a family with the harsh reality of his involvement in criminal acts.

I was horrified by the thought of someone having a family, especially with a young daughter, while also being involved in such terrible activities. It left me utterly confused. I could not help but wonder: How could a person who seemed to care about their own family get involved in such serious crimes?

Looking at the picture of him and his little daughter, I pondered what kind of life she would live. Many of the traffickers we met in later operations were not only trafficking other children, but some were also *trafficking their own family members*. This man was not selling his daughter yet, but he very well might sometime in the future if we did not shut down his operation.

A translation of some of his texts includes the following:

- "I know God brought you to me, so I will have the money I want for this project."
- "I have the children if you have the money, I will be your brother forever."
- "The young virgins were a surprise for you, but Javier already told you."
- "It is a bit risky for your guests to bring the ten- and eleven-year-olds. Children at that age cry."
- "The sex hotel will be a good business with very good profits."
- **"I know that God sent you to me."**

As I read his texts, a divine realization came upon me, a powerful acknowledgment that resonated deep within my soul: *He is right! God did send me!*

However, it became clear that the divine intervention he anticipated was far from the despicable outcomes he hoped for. A smile crossed my face as the irony in that sentence sank in. He believed God was on his side, but he was about to encounter the true Divine force that would bring his entire operation crashing down.

Now, with unwavering faith and God's guidance, our mission was set to unfold. We were not just combating a trafficking network; we were part of a grander plan to bring justice and hope to the innocent. The trafficker's words, intended to manipulate, only solidified my determination. This mission was more than a rescue; it was a divine calling to end the suffering and restore humanity to those cruelly stripped of it.

In the quiet observation that followed, the urgency of our mission took on new significance. *We will do it for that little girl's safety in Eduar's backseat.* The innocence captured in that photograph became a driving force behind my determination to shut down his enterprise, providing a future where she could grow up in a nurturing environment, free from the threats of a father entangled in the exploitation of children. My resolve was fueled by compassion, a commitment to protect the vulnerable, and a clear understanding that our actions could reshape the course of an innocent life.

As the weight of our responsibility settled upon my mind, I envisioned a ripple effect extending beyond the immediate objectives of the mission. It was not just about shutting down a criminal enterprise; it was about creating ripples of positive change that would resonate through the lives of the victims and their families. I felt a deep sense of purpose, knowing this mission was about justice and paving the way for a future where innocence could flourish and the chains of slavery could be forever broken.

One of the other photos Eduar sent me included a picture of Jesus in the background. It was a strange and unsettling sight. Here was a man hurting innocent people for his own gain, yet he had an image of Jesus, a symbol of love and forgiveness. It made me wonder about Eduar's hypocrisy. The idea of a trafficker, someone causing so much pain, having a picture of ultimate goodness and mercy, was almost too much to handle.

Over the past decade, we have encountered many traffickers who openly display religious symbols. Some have tattoos of Christian crosses and carry rosary beads. Others place Buddha statues in their homes or wear bracelets featuring the Muslim crescent moon and a star. The contradiction between their actions and the principles of peace and love taught by these religions leaves me confused.

I would expect that people engaged in such evil pursuits would choose to embrace satanic representations. Yet, the presence of Christian and Muslim symbols suggested a strange relationship between their actions and their professed beliefs. Were they trying to use religion as a way to anchor themselves to a moral compass?

It made me wonder if their outward display of religious symbols was an attempt to cover up their guilt or to fill an emptiness inside. Maybe they thought that showing off their religious beliefs could convince others, and perhaps themselves, that they were good people despite their terrible deeds. Seeing such a contrast between their actions and the religious symbols they displayed was confusing and unsettling.

I have seen the same hypocrisy with many of my associates over the years, including some who claim to be fighting trafficking. They are quick to talk about their religious beliefs, yet their actions do not match the principles they profess. This conflict between what they say they believe and how they treat others raises important questions about religious convictions. We all must consider this as we reflect on our beliefs and actions. Are we genuinely following sound moral principles, or are we twisting these principles to justify our behavior?

The importance of each of us taking a stand became increasingly evident in the ongoing battle between good and evil. We should all cling to the hope that there are enough people of moral courage to win this war. This is not a political or religious issue. It is a collective call for humanity to unite in the fight against the darkness overtaking our moral principles.

9

DIVINE INTERVENTION

Answering the Prayer of the Children

Three weeks had passed since my initial meeting with alleged traffickers, each day bringing me closer to a pivotal moment: my return to Colombia for a child rescue operation that would completely change my life and eventually set humanity on a new course. This extensive operation spanned three separate cities and required hundreds of support personnel. We held pre-operation meetings where plans were carefully laid out before returning to Colombia. Our team included cameramen, a substantial security force, and other undercover operators, all dedicated to the mission.

The security team's pedigree was outstanding: men of valor and commitment. Dave Lopez, a former Navy SEAL, led the rescue team in Medellin, Colombia, with unparalleled experience in high-stakes missions. In Cartagena, JR, another former Special Forces operator, ensured our safety with unwavering precision. These men were not just highly trained; they were elite. Their backgrounds included counter-terrorism operations, SWAT team training across the United States, and Special Response Teams for the Department of Homeland Security. With such exceptional warriors by our side, our protection was nothing short of ironclad.

In the lead-up, the pre-op team met with their counterparts in the US agencies and the Colombian federal police. The Colombian

61

CTI, known as the Technical Investigation Team, committed forty federal agents to partake in the sting operation while contacts from the US government undertook remote surveillance. Notably, Augustus joined the operation, choosing to witness it firsthand. Because of his involvement, he would play an essential role in supporting legislative changes in the United States to combat child trafficking.

The rescue operation would be on a secluded island near Colombia's Caribbean Islas de Rosario. Operational security was a top priority, with the suspects deliberately kept unaware of the exact location of the purported "party." The traffickers were told the party needed to be very private because the buyer (Pablo) was worried about the police finding out. So, for security reasons, the exact location, whether a lavish resort, an opulent house, or, in this case, a private island, would only be revealed on the day of the gathering.

The selected property featured a spacious *cabaña* topped with a palm/straw roof, complete with hammocks and beds to serve as the room where children would be separated from their perpetrators upon arrival. Furnished with a boat dock, an outdoor kitchen area, and a sizable table for negotiations with the traffickers, the property was strategically chosen to fulfill the mission's requirements.

To enhance the illusion of an ongoing drunken party, cases of beer were brought in, and the team poured the alcohol into the ocean and scattered empty bottles around to create the appearance of an ongoing party. A few Colombian agents, initially concerned about wasting good beer, volunteered to help dispose of it in the traditional way—by ingesting it! After drinking a few six-packs, their contributions to the operation decreased. Still, their enthusiastic effort to help dispose of the beer added a moment of humor to the intense preparations.

Recognizing the need to document the crimes without subjecting the children to courtroom testimony, covert cameras were strategically positioned throughout the property. I was informed that these recordings, intended as necessary evidence, would be submitted to the Colombian prosecutor's office. It would be essential to have direct conversations with the traffickers on camera to ensure they could not make claims they were unaware of the true nature of their actions.

Joseph, our Krav Maga expert, accompanied another operator to the mainland to retrieve the suspects and their victims. For Joseph, this moment was a shocking reminder of how widespread child trafficking was in that area. Recalling the scene vividly, he remarked, "I came to understand the magnitude of the problem when I saw our two large boats, the size of buses, loaded with dozens of children."

To minimize the potential risk to the children and our team during the sting operation, they informed the traffickers that we wanted to enjoy a carefree party with our friends—no weapons, no knives, no issues. Joseph personally ensured compliance, removing weapons from the traffickers and even checking the girls' purses to rule out any concealed weapons. The victims, along with their captors, were loaded onto the boats, beginning the journey to the island.

Joseph tells how many of the victims exhibited signs of being drugged by the traffickers to suppress their anxiety regarding the upcoming horror. They knew they were being transported to where the unthinkable would happen.

What transpired next was the last thing Joseph would have ever expected. About halfway to the island, one of the older teenagers took charge, urging the others to be silent and gathering the other children together. He encouraged them to join hands and, bowing his head, initiated a heartfelt prayer.

The noise on the boat prevented Joseph from catching the words of the prayer, leaving room for imagination about the thoughts and emotions racing through the hearts and minds of those young victims. The older teen, who knew all too well the harsh reality of trafficking, showed sensitivity to the fear that the younger ones were feeling. Desperate, he prayed for divine mercy, his plea echoing in the face of the approaching tragedy.

Little did the children know their prayer had been answered before the first word was uttered. Numerous undercover operators, motivated by an internal calling, had responded to the mission, committing to be on the island when the boats arrived.

Most operators' selfless dedication would never be publicly recognized, and their commitment went far beyond any desire for recognition. They simply aimed to leverage their skills and resources to bring the children to safety.

In the movie "*Sound of Freedom*," actor Bill Camp played the character Vampiro, based on an actual operator we called Batman. Although Batman was not part of this specific mission, his background of working with the cartel and his deep motivation for protecting innocence were elements we felt were essential to include in the film. Batman's story provided a compelling and authentic glimpse into the complex world of undercover operations and the personal sacrifices made by those dedicated to fighting child trafficking. By incorporating his character into the cinematic storyline, we aimed to honor the real-life heroes who risk their lives to save these kids from unimaginable horrors.

One of the most emotional lines by his character in the film is, "When God tells you to do something, you do not hesitate."

Even with the different religious backgrounds among the operators, a common thread bound them together. When asked to combat child trafficking, there was an overwhelming sense of responsibility to employ whatever talents and resources they possessed, driven by a shared commitment to rescue these vulnerable children.

Our dedicated team anxiously waited on the island, scanning the horizon until the silhouette of two boats emerged, each carrying the traffickers and their frightened victims. The moment was surreal, and the success of our carefully crafted plan was unfolding before us. The anticipation gave way to intense relief. The first step of the strategy had worked! The traffickers believed our story and had brought all their children.

As the boats smoothly docked, a wave of emotion washed over me. The arrival of fifty-four boys and girls on the edge of liberation from the clutches of trafficking marked an essential turning point in our mission. About half the victims were children; the other half looked like older teenagers, but all of them were being manipulated, controlled, and trafficked by these monsters. It was important to keep the victims safe during the sting operation. We needed to separate them swiftly and effectively from the traffickers.

Due to the victim's pre-existing trauma, it would be important to shield them from potentially upsetting scenes, such as witnessing the money changing hands or the upcoming police intervention aimed at arresting the perpetrators. Our primary concern was to spare them from any additional emotional distress.

We explained to the traffickers our desire for a private meeting, assuring them our female counterparts would assist in preparing the kids for the upcoming event. Such arrangements were pretty standard in situations like these, where perpetrators often brought females to groom the victims before the party. Unknown to the traffickers, however, these women were not just ordinary participants; they were highly trained operatives committed to safeguarding the children at all costs.

Among the female operators, one had received extensive training from my Krav Maga instructor, Joseph. I clearly remember sparring with her years ago. I made a joking comment, saying she "hit like a girl." Despite her small size, weighing just ninety pounds, she quickly showed her skill by putting me in a "Rear Naked Choke," forcing me to tap out before I lost consciousness. This humbling experience highlighted the exceptional abilities of these women, ensuring that the children were in very capable and protective hands.

We felt a sense of relief as the victims were guided away from the traffickers and into the shelter of the cabaña. Here, they were given candies and drinks in an effort to provide some peace to their deeply traumatized souls. Little did they realize their time of liberation was close at hand, and this separation from their captors was the beginning of their journey toward healing and recovery.

Among the perpetrators present were those we had previously met with at the restaurant, along with an additional trafficker who had brought even more victims. The group of criminals included the ominous presence of the female trafficker, the beauty queen Linda, dressed in a bright yellow dress. She seemed ready to supervise the meeting. Eduar, the businessman with disturbing plans to transform his property into a sex hotel, was well-groomed, sporting a clean-shaven look and a crisp white polo shirt.

Dressed in a sleek, black outfit, I deliberately chose my attire, representing the dark identity central to my undercover role. What I found intriguing was the unexpected similarities in the clothes worn by many of the traffickers—Fuego, Samuel, and the new suspect were all wearing black. This peculiar alignment added an eerie layer to the unfolding scene, emphasizing the evil nature of the operation we would dismantle.

Among the group who had come down from the US for the operation was Cassius's church bishop. He stood there, watching the heartbreaking sight of trafficked victims being led off the boat and towards the cabaña. Fuego, one of the traffickers, stood casually beside him as if this horrific scene was nothing out of the ordinary. For us, seeing this was deeply disturbing, a harsh reminder of the brutal reality of human trafficking. But to Fuego, it was just another day of selling trafficked children and another event in a long string of terrible decisions.

Engaging in conversation with the church leader, Fuego casually mentioned how he gave some of the victim's cocaine that morning so they would not cry during the ordeal. He coldly pointed at one of the girls, making explicit remarks about her and shamelessly joking about the unspeakable acts one could commit. It was a twisted display of indifference to him as if such behavior were par for the course in his world.

Filled with a potent mix of outrage and righteous indignation towards Fuego, the church leader, now a fervent witness to the unfolding tragedy, held an unwavering belief that justice would soon catch up with these traffickers. With a conviction that transcended the unsettling scene before him, he approached one of the other operators and, in a hushed tone, declared, "Fuego is F##ked." This outburst of vulgarity from a religious leader highlighted how all of us were feeling, having a steadfast belief that the perpetrators of these heinous acts would soon face the consequences they deserved.

Three weeks before, when Fuego showed me the picture of the eleven-year-old girl they called Princess, it solidified my commitment to rescue her. Now, seeing all the children in person made my dedication even stronger. The heartbreaking sight of the victims getting off the boat and entering the cabaña will stay in my memory forever.

A wave of strong emotions hit me as I wondered where these kids came from. Were they taken from good homes? Did they come from broken families? Were they runaways from bad situations at home? The harsh reality of trafficking was alarming to witness.

It became clear that many of the victims had been given drugs by the traffickers, and some seemed barely aware of what was happening. Witnessing this heartbreaking abuse stirred such a deep feeling of empathy and sorrow in me that I had to fight back tears. The children's vulnerability and the harsh circumstances they faced highlighted the urgency of our mission to rescue and protect them from further harm.

The traffickers were ushered to an outdoor table adjacent to the cabaña building, where discussions unfolded regarding the party and details about each of the children. I was invited to occupy the prominent position at the head of the table. Unbeknownst to the traffickers, standing guard behind me was my long-time friend, Augustus, operating incognito and bearing the covert alias *La Sombra*, aptly translating to "The Shadow." His presence not only added an extra layer of security, but he would go on to share the rescue story in ways that would help change international law.

Seated and assuming the role of the host of this despicable party, I began to establish an atmosphere of ease and friendship. I expressed my gratitude and admiration to the traffickers for bringing all the promised children to the party, hinting at the possibility of a successful business partnership. The carefully chosen words were meant to create an illusion of cooperation, hiding the true purpose of the upcoming operation.

Mixed within our team, strategically placed Colombian federal agents acted as our local staff, adding a level of security to the negotiations. The plan involved these undercover agents quietly watching the party. Once we had enough recorded evidence to expose the traffickers, a secret radio signal from the undercover waiters would call in Colombia's Navy and Coast Guard, who were waiting for the right moment to come in for the arrests.

The undercover Colombian federal agents took on the roles of maids, waiters, and cooks. However, their lack of culinary skills became evident, nearly blowing their cover. Once, their attempt to serve a cheese plate almost gave them away when they presented a large uncut block of cheese without any utensils, knives, or plates for sharing. This mistake could have raised suspicions, but the traffickers were too focused on discussing the money for their project. We humorously reflect on the incident, noting, *"They were not very good cooks, but they were well-armed!"*

On the island's far side, an additional group of twenty-five Colombian special agents remained strategically stationed on boats, ready for action as they awaited the signal to initiate a coordinated sting operation.

The plan was carefully laid out. Once our team ensured that all the victims were safely protected and had obtained critical confessions from each suspect, captured on hidden cameras for prosecution, we would initiate the sting operation. The chosen cue for swift action would be ordering Tequila, a covert signal to keep the traffickers unaware of the impending storm.

When our team instructed the waiters to bring Tequila, marking the start of the anticipated party, the waiters, fully aware of the secret plan, would return to the kitchen. There, they would swiftly radio the Colombian operators stationed on the boats, signaling them to commence the well-coordinated raid on the party.

10

THE GIFTS I BROUGHT YOU

Truth in the Eyes of a Princess

The upcoming minutes were critical as our focus shifted to gathering incriminating evidence from the traffickers. We needed to capture each of them on video, explaining how they obtained the victims, what services they were offering for our party, and how far they were willing to exploit these innocent lives. These conversations would be difficult but necessary for prosecution. It was essential to avoid alerting the traffickers that their every word was being recorded.

This delicate task required a careful approach. Every word spoken and each question asked had to be precise. The objective was twofold: maintain the appearance of an ordinary conversation while skillfully extracting incriminating details. We needed to secure essential information for legal action while ensuring the traffickers remained unaware of the hidden cameras to ensure the success of our mission.

We began the conversation by handing envelopes to the traffickers, each labeled with their name. This act of accepting money for exploiting the victims was captured on undercover cameras, providing necessary evidence for prosecutors.

The act of receiving payment served two purposes: it gave the traffickers a false sense of security and recorded their compliance on camera. This visual proof of their involvement would be vital for their prosecution and imprisonment.

When we presented the envelopes, we explained to the traffickers that this marked the initial compensation for their role in bringing forth the children. We assured them that the remainder of their compensation would be rewarded at the end of the party, contingent upon all my guests' satisfaction.

The traffickers reacted differently. Some carefully took the money out of the envelopes, counting the bills, while others showed an air of confidence as they casually put the envelopes in their pockets. This financial transaction set the stage for the upcoming conversation.

Suddenly, a loud thud broke the silence. One of the hidden cameras had fallen to the ground with an alarming crash. In that heart-stopping moment, we all knew the potential danger this incident posed to our covert operation. Fear gripped me and the other operators as we worried the traffickers might have noticed.

Luckily, the traffickers were too busy counting the money to notice the noise. This unexpected stroke of luck meant that our mission remained safe, and we could continue our pursuit of justice without being exposed.

Then, the dark and challenging discussion began. Our goal was to gather detailed information from each suspect, convincing them to disclose the identities of those they had brought, their ages, and the nature of the exploitative services they intended to facilitate. The suspects revealed details about some of the victims in a conversation similar to this:

"Rose is 14; she is from Argentina. We have had her for three years, and she is trained to do anything your guests want."

"Teddy is from Honduras; he is our smallest."

"We call the pretty one Princess; she is eleven years old and is still a virgin. She is the one with long braids."

The traffickers talked about the victims with disturbing ease, treating them like objects instead of human beings. Their casual attitude during this degrading conversation was infuriating. Clearly, these kinds of talks were typical for them, repeated countless times without remorse. Even with the upsetting nature of the conversation, there was a glimmer of hope, knowing this would be the last time they would have such gut-wrenching discussions before going to prison.

Deep gratitude filled our operators as we experienced mixed emotions, knowing our team was protecting these vulnerable victims. The seriousness of the situation and our responsibility highlighted the difference between those who commit such evil and those who work to stop it. In moments of reflection, I wondered: What kind of world allows such evil to exist? This question reminded me how important it is to fight against this darkness. Our intervention was meant to be a light of hope and justice amid the darkness.

Unexpectedly, Eduar, the businessman trafficker who had previously texted, "I know God sent you to me," abruptly stood up and exclaimed, "Pablo, I must show you the gifts I brought for you!"

Assuredly, he disappeared into the building where the victims were confined. Within a few minutes, the troubling sound of crying children could be heard from within the cabaña building. These were not cries of physical harm but rather the distressing sounds of unimaginable fear.

The urge to intervene was overwhelming as every instinct screamed to go inside and see what was wrong. However, we knew that any sudden move could jeopardize the entire mission. The traffickers were still unaware of our true intentions, and maintaining that secrecy was crucial for the operation's success. Despite the emotional strain and the desperate need to act, we remained in our seats, calming ourselves to maintain the facade. This restraint, though challenging, was necessary to ensure the traffickers would be caught and brought to justice, ultimately saving the children from ever having to experience this again.

Ignoring the temptation to send someone to check on the victims, we decided to stay put, trusting the female operators who were with them. These skilled professionals, trained to handle challenging situations, gave us confidence in their ability to manage the emotional unrest coming from inside the building.

The children, overwhelmed with fear, believed this was the dreaded moment when their innocence would be violently stripped away. Their crying was precisely what the female trafficker at the restaurant was worried about, who had stated, "I can't bring the virgins because if I do, they might cry." Her concern was now becoming real in the cries coming from the victims.

Nearly ten minutes later, Eduar reappeared from the building, escorting four victims, all virgins, three young girls, and one little boy, all visibly trembling with fear. The boy, taken from his home in Haiti, was one of the kids Fuego had given cocaine to earlier in the day based on his twisted idea that it would take away the child's anxiety about potential harm.

As I saw their fear, I wondered: *What kind of monster would ever find this attractive?*

One of the girls immediately caught my attention, and a powerful wave of recognition washed over me. It was the same eleven-year-old girl whom Fuego had showcased to me on his phone during our visit to the restaurant, the one they had heartlessly referred to as Princess. Her picture had galvanized my commitment to help fund this rescue. She was portrayed as the focal point of the *Sound of Freedom* movie, where she was rescued from the jungle. Yet, in the real story, she was brought by the traffickers to the island with the other children, desperately needing protection.

Princess, as the traffickers referred to her, had long braids flowing down her back. She was wearing a shirt decorated with pink letters and a kitten drawing. The innocence in her face and clothing added a layer of deep sadness to the unfolding situation.

The choice of clothing, the intricacy of her braids, and the genuine innocence reflected in her eyes all stood as emotional reminders of the stolen youth these traffickers heartlessly exploited. At that moment, the contrast between her appearance and her terrible situation showed how urgently she needed help before her innocence was taken away.

The trafficker coldheartedly positioned "Princess" before me. As I sat on a chair, her tiny stature became pronounced, barely surpassing my seated height as she was standing up. It was a distressing sight. The traffickers had covered her innocent face with an excessive amount of makeup, now marred by streaks of tears. The residue of her unrestrained crying spoke volumes of the fear that gripped her, an overwhelming terror coming from the belief that I, the man before her, was the monster ready to violate her. Everything about her appearance painted an emotional picture of the trauma she had endured, a powerful reminder of the urgent need to tear down the wicked forces exploiting innocence for their perverse purposes.

My heart pounded with an overwhelming intensity, a flood of emotions surging through me. My compassionate heart desperately wanted to reassure her, to promise her safety and a reunion with her parents. But the words caught in my throat, the weight of the unspoken promise pressing heavily against my chest.

Instead, I gently grasped her trembling hands and asked a simple question, "Como te llamas?" What is your name? This question held deep meaning, recognizing that "Princess" was the name given to her by her captors. It was just another act of sarcasm as they were in the process of selling her innocence.

Her inability to answer spoke volumes, evidence of the psychological captivity she endured. I could sense her internal struggle, trying to decide what response the traffickers wanted her to disclose. As I peered into her eyes, registering the intense fear reflecting back at me, a transformative realization began. In that emotional exchange, the world seemed to stand still. It was a soul-defining moment that created an unwavering determination within me.

With unspoken assurance, I softly uttered, "Está bien." (It is okay) The statement was more than words; it was an unwavering promise. In that sacred moment, a solemn vow formed within my soul, a pledge not only to this vulnerable child before me but also to myself and God to be a powerful force to liberate innocent souls around the world from the evil clutches of trafficking. I would dedicate my life to fiercely confront and eradicate such evil from the face of the earth. God's children and their innocence are not for sale!

In that crucial moment, I almost shattered our carefully crafted cover as a flood of emotions threatened to take over. A lump formed in my throat, and tears pressed against my eyes. Staying composed while undercover was incredibly tough, especially when we had to hide our true feelings from the traffickers. Holding back the intense emotions inside was a struggle, but we all knew that any slip could ruin everything.

Turning to Eduar, I urged, "Please escort her and the other kids back into the cabaña. We intend to continue discussing business for a while longer. But thank you for allowing me this glimpse into the party. I must say, I am genuinely speechless by the models you have showcased."

With our mission on the brink of success, we possessed the essential components for legal action. The suspects, unknowingly captured on camera, had clearly confessed to their despicable plans of profiting from the children's innocence and the methods used in acquiring the victims, providing authorities with the necessary evidence for their incarceration.

With all the incriminating evidence secured, it was time to summon the troops and end this disgusting ordeal. The predetermined signal for the sting would be the code word "Tequila." This signal served as the cue to call in the specialized strike team. So, we calmly ordered Tequila, setting in motion the events that would lead to the arrest of these traffickers!

11

THE DEADLIEST 45 MINUTES

Delaying the Darkness: A Business Deal with the Devil

Once the covert signal was given, our anticipation heightened as we expected swift and decisive action from the Colombian federal agents. Armed with an abundance of incriminating evidence against the traffickers and with the children securely tucked away in the protective confines of the cabaña, the stage was set for the enforcement of justice. It was a critical moment demanding immediate and coordinated intervention.

The minutes following the Tequila order became a frightening and nerve-wracking passage of time. Five minutes ticked away with no sign of the Colombian agents. Since we had concluded the financial transactions and conversations about their plans for the children, the order of Tequila unintentionally misled the traffickers into believing the party was ready to begin.

In line with commencing the long-awaited party, Fuego produced his stash of cocaine for all present, prompting the other traffickers to rise from their seats to bring the children out for the planned sex party with our undercover operatives—a situation we could not allow to unfold! The victims needed to remain secure within the cabaña.

The Colombian special operations team needed to strike immediately. "Operation go, go, go!" echoed through our minds as we anxiously awaited the coordinated action. Yet, a feeling of uncertainty hung in the air. Where were the federal agents when we needed them most?

We were in a very dangerous situation. Our primary concern was ensuring the safety of the children while strategically stalling the traffickers. What happened next unfolded as an unmistakable act of divine intervention. Leveraging my extensive experience negotiating numerous business transactions throughout my career, I recognized the urgent need to employ these skills immediately. An inner prompting guided me to utilize my business training to divert the traffickers' focus, sustaining their attention until the Colombian agents arrived.

As Linda, Samuel, and Eduar were on the verge of retrieving the victims, I quickly intervened, urging them to stop. "Guys, hold on a moment! If you unleash that cocaine and bring out those kids, we will have the wildest party and be in a stupor for days. I have only just managed to regain some sobriety from last night's party; let's capitalize on this opportunity. You have proven your ability to deliver on your promises with over fifty children. How about we sketch out a business plan right here, right now?"

I requested that someone fetch me a piece of paper and writing utensils. A notebook and pen were promptly brought to me. I proceeded to conduct an interview with the traffickers, inadvertently crafting one of the most reprehensible business plans ever conceived by outlining the target customer, securing the supply line, and constructing cash flow models. The chilling reality of the plan, however, lay in its heinous nature, as it revolved around the exploitation of innocent children.

Augustus (La Sombra) played a crucial role undercover, doubling as both my bodyguard and translator. Thinking back, he often describes this particular assignment as the most unsettling translation he has ever been a part of. The upsetting conversation began when I proposed the topic, stating, "Let's talk about your inventory, the children. For this business plan to thrive, I must understand your sources and the potential for additional supply. What is the cost of acquiring a young Colombian girl? Is it comparable to obtaining a boy?"

I carefully noted the figures, settling on a sum in the few thousand dollars range. Continuing the inquiry, I asked another question: "And what about a young blonde American girl?" The response was nearly ten times higher because of the increased difficulty of acquisition and the challenges associated with crossing borders.

Inquiring about the details of the business, I asked for clarification on any additional expenses associated with preparing the victims for their eventual sale and the timeframe for them to be ready for a party like this.

Linda, the former beauty queen turned trafficker, responded, "The immediate sale of the children is not possible; you heard those girls crying. We need funds to provide food and lodging as we prepare them before selling."

The fact that they understood these kinds of details sent chills down my spine, creating a feeling of disgust. The wicked nature of their business plan became increasingly apparent, and I found it challenging to hide my discomfort during this troubling conversation. Regardless of my inner turmoil, we had to persist in prolonging the discussion until the federal agents arrived while the victims remained safely within the confines of the house.

It became important to shift the conversation away from the distressing focus on the children to preserve my own mental well-being. Expressing my intention, I redirected the discussion toward probing into their revenue plans, beginning with a comprehensive understanding of their customer base. They proceeded to inform me about a seemingly endless stream of narcissistic, affluent Americans who frequented Cartagena to engage in sex tourism.

Shockingly, many of these deranged buyers expressed a particular interest in the underaged models they were selling. Firm in their belief of a never-ending demand, they proposed the idea of charging a substantial $100,000 annual membership fee for exclusive access to their resort. The fact that they believed there was that kind of demand prompted me to dive deeper into the details of their morally despicable business model.

Throughout the majority of my life, my notion of a pedophile was that of an overweight, middle-aged man with unkempt, greasy hair—a solitary loser addicted to pornography, residing in his mother's basement. I could not understand why any successful politician, actor, or businessman enjoying a life of abundance and excess wealth would willingly choose to utilize their money to cause harm to children.

I continued questioning the traffickers to understand their client base. Where was this demand coming from? We also needed to extend the conversation, hoping the federal agents would arrive at any time. More than fifteen minutes had passed, and the strike team was still nowhere in sight! How long could we keep stalling?

I inquired about their typical approach when confronted with children who cried, as they had earlier that day. I hoped to detect any glimmer of compassion within the hearts of these criminals. Unfortunately, their response was utterly void of empathy, suggesting their typical solution was to administer cocaine to pacify the kids.

Sensing my hint of uneasiness surrounding the crying children, they quickly changed the subject and resumed discussing the vast profits they anticipated. The conversation reeked of unbridled greed, leaving no room for even the slightest consideration of the lives that their actions would inevitably shatter.

I returned to the spreadsheet aspect of our conversation, attempting to stall by inquiring about the project's cash flow projections. The startling reality that this despicable business plan appeared financially viable due to the relentless demand from American clients left me feeling queasy. I pressed on, recognizing the importance of gathering intelligence for future undercover operations.

I asked, "How frequently can you sell one of your models daily? On average, what is the ideal age of the models when you bring them into the trade? How many years can you sell them, and what is the protocol for dealing with them once they become too old?" The responses were sickening. Every word of the conversation was disturbing, but all I could think of was, "*Where are the federal agents? What could have gone wrong?*"

Continuing to draw out the conversation, the focus shifted to the virgins they had paraded in front of us moments before, pretending to be interested in the financial details of their cash flow model. I remarked, "So, for the older virgin, you are charging me a few thousand dollars and even more for the younger one. Is this the standard pricing, or are you charging me a premium because I have money? Do not lie to me; what is the usual price range for these?"

One of the traffickers reassured me, saying, "No, Jefe, we are not trying to deceive you. That is the exact amount we charge for the zero-kilometer models."

Zero-kilometers! I screamed the phrase in my mind, feeling a wave of horror as they referred to these children as if they were commodities comparable to vehicles or any other lifeless objects for sale. *Can the sting operation happen immediately, please? These criminals need to go to prison now!*

I pressed on, pretending to be interested in the details of their illicit operation. "Alright, following the initial $2,000 for a virgin, what are you able to sell her for after that? Does it decrease to $500 each or perhaps $200 each time?" As I carefully documented their business plan, Linda uttered something so horrific that you might prefer to skip the following few paragraphs.

To my utter horror, she declared, "Oh, we can sell them as a virgin many times over."

My confusion grew, and I demanded clarification, "What do you mean?" I paused, my pen hovering over the paper as I transcribed this unsettling conversation into the fabricated business plan. How could they possibly market them as virgins more than once?

Linda's chilling answer: "It only costs about $200 for a procedure to sew back their hymen..." The horrific revelation hung heavily in the air, emphasizing the terrible reality of child trafficking.

The shock of what I was hearing was beyond comprehension. She was discussing unimaginable horrors with a detachment that chilled me to the bone.

The traffickers, showing no emotion, casually talked about the most horrifying scenarios imaginable. The terrible nature of their conversation left me struggling to understand the reality in front of me. In what twisted world does such cruelty exist? How deep into evil must someone digress to think up and commit such awful acts?

What about the complicit doctors willing to perform these surgeries? Did any of these people possess even a shred of conscience? These questions echoed in my mind, each a stark reminder of the unimaginable darkness behind their operations.

"God help humanity!" echoed within me, capturing the sheer horror and disbelief at the depravity unfolding before my eyes and ears. The air grew thick, and a sense of suffocation overcame me. If only for a moment, I had to halt this conversation to catch my breath and try to understand the magnitude of the evil we had just been exposed to.

Twenty-five minutes had elapsed since Tequila was ordered and the commencement of a terrible conversation that was never meant to occur. The anticipated federal raid on the party should have happened long ago, yet there was no sign of their arrival. The atmosphere grew increasingly tense. All we could do in this dangerous situation was buy time, praying and hoping the federal agents would eventually make their long-awaited appearance. The uncertainty of the delay made the situation even more severe.

Struggling to maintain my composure in the face of such wickedness, I shifted my focus to the logistical aspects of their vile enterprise. "Linda and Samuel," I began, attempting to adopt a more business-like tone, "let's discuss the operations of your modeling company. How many models do you currently control? What methods do you use to convince parents to bring their children? And, on a larger scale, what are your plans to grow your enterprise?"

Linda, leveraging her established credibility as a pageant model, had been utilizing her status to lure young models into the sex trade. Diving deeper, I asked questions about their expansion plans. Linda was confident in growing the business model, proposing building a website, printing brochures, and expanding her operations to other countries.

Convinced of their ability to consistently furnish the resort with a steady stream of new children, they proposed I invest in their modeling venture in addition to the money I was committing to the sex hotel. While their project required less initial capital than the resort, they wanted an initial investment of $75,000 for phase one, anticipating additional money from me as the project unfolded. They believed this sum would adequately kickstart their operations and contribute to the overall success of the resort.

The entire operation's dependence on the toxic motivators of greed, envy, ego, and lust deeply disturbed me. The insatiable desires for wealth and perverted sex were apparent in the actions of both the traffickers and the buyers. Linda and Samuel also showed how they used the allure of money and fame to trap their unsuspecting victims.

Addressing Eduar, I suggested a shift in focus to the hotel itself. "Let's discuss the details of your resort. How expansive do you visualize it? What is the room capacity for customers? And concerning the models, where do you intend to house them when they are not engaged with customers? Additionally, what other amenities are you planning?" As we engaged in this nauseating discussion, I began sketching the layout with the traffickers, working on cost estimations for the construction.

Even with my professional background in business and real estate, having been involved in designing everything from opulent residences to sizable office complexes and apartments, the nature of these discussions on a project with such alarming intentions was inexcusable. Grateful for the certainty this project would never come to fruition, I wrestled with the disgust of even talking about such a venture. My focus shifted to finding other ways to prolong the conversation, anxiously awaiting the arrival of Colombian agents. The question on all of the operators' minds was: Where were the agents?

More than half an hour had passed since we gave the covert signal by ordering Tequila. The federal agents still had not arrived. Our anxiety heightened with each passing moment, as the absence of enforcement raised concerns about potential complications or unforeseen obstacles. I was nearly running out of strategies to extend the discussion in an attempt to delay the party with the victims.

One of the operatives maintained a connection with a group of people back home who were closely monitoring the progress of the sting operation. During this dangerous phase, a group chat comprised of numerous supporters back home was actively engaged. Our team remained in the dark about the unfolding events and the reasons behind the delay. In a moment of desperation, the operator stepped away from the table and sent a single word to the group: PRAY.

At that point, nothing short of divine intervention could save these children. All we could do was hope for a miracle. We knew that *if there was ever a time to ask for God's help, this would be it.* Our hearts were filled with desperation, but we held on to a flicker of hope that somehow, amid this darkness, an intervention would occur and deliver these innocent lives from unimaginable evil.

All we could do was delay, and I was running out of questions to ask about the business plan. In a desperate attempt to stop the despicable conversation around exploiting innocence, I changed the focus to the contract itself.

I addressed the traffickers, stating, "Let's take this discussion to the next level. We understand your vision for this project. It is evident you have created a steady supply of inventory for the resort; you clearly understand your market and have created a plan for a profitable business that promises millions in annual returns. I am willing to proceed with the investment, but on the condition that I have complete control with a 55 percent stake. The remaining 45 percent must be distributed among the rest of you."

Recognizing Eduar's key role in orchestrating the plan, I proposed a share distribution, suggesting he receive a 30 percent stake while the remaining members could divide the remaining 15 percent. I immediately saw anger arise in Linda and the other traffickers, who were expecting a larger piece of the business.

I then encouraged them to discuss the arrangement with each other and finalize the numbers right then and there. "Why don't you guys hash it out, and then let's formalize the deal on paper? I am ready to draft this agreement and sign right now," I declared, seeking to push the negotiation forward. Almost instantly, a heated argument broke out among the traffickers as they strongly disagreed about what they believed they deserved.

When dealing with people with unbridled, arrogant egos and no regard for the sanctity of life, a dispute over money can quickly turn into a fierce and ruthless battle. The table became an arena of conflicting interests, with each trafficker passionately demanding a larger share. My strategy, designed to stir conflict and extend the discussions, was the perfect choice. The purposeful delay proved to be a tactical success as the contention grew, driven by hostility and fierce competition.

Finally, an agonizing *forty-five minutes* after the signal for the raid was given, just as the dispute reached a fever pitch, Colombian federal agents stormed the island. They descended upon the scene from all directions, encircling the property with guns drawn and voices raised in unison, commanding, "On the ground, on the ground!" The delay tactics had served their purpose, ending with a dramatic raid by Colombian police.

12

THE SOUND OF FREEDOM

The Resounding Cry of Liberation

As the federal agents flooded the secluded island, a surge of adrenaline rushed through me, with a frightening realization: It was the first time in my life when the cold, steel barrel of a loaded firearm was ominously pointed in my direction. Little did I realize this marked the beginning of many similar experiences

Over the following decade, numerous rescue operations ended in similar scenarios. Federal police, armed and yelling, would storm in, ordering everyone to drop to the ground. We had to convince traffickers in different cities that we were also being arrested and would be sent to the USA to face trial. Because of this, we found ourselves surrounded by many firearms carried by federal agents who were usually on our side throughout the operation.

Over the years, our undercover work put us in some extremely dangerous situations. We weren't just dealing with traffickers; we also had to face corrupt law enforcement officers who were secretly working for the criminals. In these cases, every decision mattered because one wrong move could have exposed our entire operation.

There were also tense moments when we were arrested by honest local police officers who didn't know we were working with the federal government. These encounters were a harsh reminder that danger could come from anywhere, and it was hard to know who to trust.

In the initial sting operation, a group of Colombian CTI agents quickly stormed the scene. Augustus, positioned behind me, played the role of La Sombra, acting as my bodyguard for our undercover mission. He ushered me away from the chaos, casting himself as my protector. He guided me to the ground in a calculated move, making our fake scenario look real. Together, we lay face down on the sand while the federal agents questioned the traffickers near the table.

With the scorching heat of the sand burning our faces and ants crawling over our bodies, we quickly realized we should have chosen a more comfortable spot to wait out the traffickers' interrogation. The hot sand made our position nearly unbearable, but the relief of not having to continue the sickening conversation with the criminals made the physical discomfort worthwhile. As we lay there, we could hear the agents questioning the traffickers, their voices a blend of authority and frustration.

Despite the unpleasant conditions, we knew it was a small price to pay for the federal agents to arrive and finally take the criminals into custody. Our discomfort was temporary, but the operation's impact would be life-changing for the victims who had finally been liberated. The scorching heat seemed insignificant compared to the joy and relief of knowing that innocent lives were being saved. Each bead of sweat was a reminder of the sacrifices made to bring justice. The thought of families being reunited and children gaining freedom filled us with a deep feeling of purpose and fulfillment. Our temporary suffering was nothing compared to the lasting freedom and hope we were helping to restore to those who had been in the bonds of modern-day slavery.

The arrival of the Colombian agents brought an overwhelming sense of relief, freeing us from the intense and brutal negotiations with the traffickers. The forty-five-minute delay felt endless, leaving me both physically exhausted and mentally drained. At forty-three, this day stood out as one of the most significant in my life, sparking a journey that would forever change my understanding of my purpose.

The weight of the experience lingered, leaving a lasting impression on my heart and propelling me into a new phase of life filled with deep reflection and a reevaluation of my beliefs. It was a moment of profound change, one that shifted my priorities and convictions entirely. This experience forced me to question everything I once valued and helped me see the world through a different lens. It marked the beginning of a journey to understand myself and the world in a completely new way.

Witnessing the horrific reality of children being sold for sex left a permanent mark on my soul. As we lay face down in the sand, forced to listen to the traffickers' sickening justifications for their vile actions, a profound realization hit me. In that emotional moment, I experienced a deep, internal transformation, knowing I could never go back to who I once was. The pursuit of money and recognition that had once driven me suddenly seemed insignificant compared to the urgent need to protect these innocent lives from the grasp of such evil.

The children's cries from earlier that day echoed continually in my mind, reminding me of the abject horror inflicted upon them. In that life-changing moment, I felt an unwavering conviction that transcended this earthly existence—a firm belief in the intervention of a higher power. I could feel the power of God and all the righteous angels of the universe rallying behind our worthy cause, urging us to stand firm against the forces of darkness.

In this universal battle between good and evil, the call to protect the children became the single purpose that overshadowed all other concerns. It was a moment where the collective consciousness of virtuous beings across the universe rejoiced as brave men and women rallied to fulfill the solemn duty of shielding the innocent. This awakening served as a battle cry, uniting us in a noble effort to protect the most vulnerable among us.

The indescribable tension that gripped us in the past hour gave way to an overwhelming feeling of relief as we witnessed the safe rescue of the victims. Throughout our following rescue missions, I have often emphasized an important truth: The moment we pull these children from the depths of Hell is undeniably important, yet it is only the beginning of their difficult path toward recovery.

The real work begins after liberation. It is a true labor of love requiring time, patience, and a devoted understanding of the complex journey toward healing. The scars, both visible and hidden, require a compassionate approach extending far beyond the immediate rescue operation.

After a long and intense ordeal, we finally had a few moments to reflect on what we had experienced. The countless hours of careful planning, generous financial support from donors, and dangerous encounters with child traffickers resulted in the successful rescue of fifty-four victims in Cartagena and over 120 across three cities.

This operation was an extraordinary success in every respect. The traffickers, who had committed horrific crimes, were finally being brought to justice and were on their way to prison, where they would no longer be able to harm others. But what made this victory truly meaningful was knowing that the children were now safe. The thought that their suffering was over and that their journey to healing could finally begin was the most rewarding outcome of all. It wasn't just about capturing the criminals; it was about giving these children a chance to reclaim their lives and find the peace they deserved.

While the Colombian federal agents interrogated the traffickers, over thirty child protective services professionals arrived on the island. Although the reason for their delay was unclear, we were incredibly relieved to see these compassionate social workers ready to help the vulnerable children. They made their way into the cabaña, where the victims were kept safe from the interrogation. These dedicated aftercare teams began their critical mission of contacting the families of the victims and initiating the essential medical care and therapy needed to start the healing process.

After an intense round of questioning and the careful collection of evidence, the traffickers were securely loaded onto one of the waiting boats and taken away from the island. As they departed, we all breathed a sigh of relief and could finally drop the act we had kept up during the operation.

Our first task was to get our belongings from a designated section of the cabaña, which had an outdoor bathroom and changing area. The grass roof allowed sounds to travel easily, letting us hear everything happening inside where the children were. I went into the room with Scott, my friend and a key supporter who helped fund the mission. As we moved from the intense atmosphere outside to the more private space, we felt the weight of the operation start to lift, and the mood began to change.

As we were retrieving our bags from the small room, an unforgettable moment happened, an auditory gift that would remain in my memory forever. Turning to Scott, I urged him to listen attentively, asking, "Can you hear that?" The room next to ours was filled with the comforting sound of Child Protective Services professionals consoling children who had just been rescued from unimaginable horrors. The genuine love and compassion in their voices were clear and deeply moving.

It was not just the caregivers' voices that resonated with us; it was the unmistakable sounds coming from the children. In the room next to ours, laughter and cheerful singing filled the air, a stark contrast to the heartbreaking crying we had heard less than an hour before. The powerful contrast between those opposing sounds moved me to tears.

In that life-altering moment, that "Sound of Freedom" became the most beautiful and memorable sound I had ever heard. It was a witness to the spirit and strength of these brave young souls who, in the face of their recent traumas, managed to find comfort and joy in the aftermath.

Although the children were not supposed to know we were the "good guys," it seemed some unspoken connection had formed with the 11-year-old girl the traffickers called Princess. Whether through the protective services group revealing our identity or simply a feeling in her heart, this child somehow understood the true nature of our mission.

As we were being led off the island, I saw her standing by the door with a group of children, her hand resting on the screen. Tears filled her eyes again as she looked at me, but this time, a soft smile lit up her face. In her imperfect but heartfelt English, she gently waved and said, "Thank you, Americans." The depth of her thankfulness was beyond expression, leaving a lasting impact on the rest of my life.

Trembling with emotion, I turned to one of the operators on our team, unable to hold back the overwhelming feelings. Choking back sobs, the words spilled out: "That was one of the most life-changing experiences I've ever had." The weight of the moment made my voice shake. "My whole career has been about chasing wealth, working hard to make the rich even richer. But now, here on this island, I've realized I want something more. I want to make a real difference, to do something that truly matters. This rescue mission has changed everything for me."

With sincerity, I asked the team, "What do you need, and how can I be a part of it?" The response was everything I had hoped for. It was explained that my unique profile and training could play a crucial role in luring criminals for future child rescue operations. One of the seasoned operators emphasized, *"If you are willing to be the bait, this will change your whole life."*

PART III

UNDERCOVER ALIAS - DOCTORS IN THE JUNGLE

13

HOW DID THEY FIND ME?

Undercover Alias Unraveled

B am bam bam! The forceful, determined knock on my front door jolted me awake from a peaceful nap. I was nestled in my luxurious home in Utah within a highly secure gated community, a world away from the traffickers we helped put behind bars. For several years following the Cartagena mission, I had led or played a crucial part in dozens of undercover child rescue operations. My carefully crafted undercover alias was supposed to be unbreakable. The team and I had been face-to-face with hundreds of criminals, with the expectation that our cover would be protected. I was confident the traffickers had no way of discovering my true identity.

Our missions had taken us from the island in Colombia to the streets of Thailand, from the beaches of Mexico to the jungles of Haiti. Because of our efforts, countless children were free, and many dangerous criminals were in prison. I was enjoying the safety of my secure home, with guards protecting every entrance. A person had somehow slipped through our security guards, who had not informed me of the visitor.

The operator on the Colombian island mission had told me that choosing to be the bait on rescue missions would change my whole life. Now, years later, that change was knocking at my door—quite literally.

As I opened the door, a towering figure stood before me, his eyes scanning the room with an unsettling intensity. "I am looking for Paul Hutchinson, also known as Paul Steel!" he said, his words carrying an edge that sent a shiver down my spine. "Paul Steel" was one of my aliases, carefully fabricated to carry out child rescue missions across Cancun, Bangkok, Tijuana, Port-au-Prince, and the Dominican Republic. Countless traffickers knew that name, but it was shielded from my home life in every way possible. The shock of my undercover identity being exposed in my own home gripped me like a vice, making me realize the danger of my situation.

My mind raced. How did they find me? Was this a hitman sent by one of the imprisoned child traffickers? A sudden vulnerability washed over me, a feeling I had not experienced in years. It was as if the ground had been pulled from under my feet, leaving me in shock and disorientation. I caught a glimpse of a handgun in a holster hidden beneath his shirt. My eyes locked onto his hands, searching for any sign he might reach for it. We had trained extensively in methods to disarm an assailant, but understanding his intentions was the crucial first step.

The man at my door stared at me with a piercing gaze as he introduced himself as an agent of the Federal Bureau of Investigation (FBI), his voice cold and detached. He identified me as Paul Hutchinson, but the mention of my alias, Paul Steel, made my blood run cold. Without breaking eye contact, he handed me a thick stack of documents. As I glanced down, my heart pounded when I saw the words "Subpoena for an FBI Grand Jury" printed boldly on the top page.

The papers felt heavy in my hands, carrying the potential to destroy my carefully constructed life. Before I could gather my thoughts to inquire further, the agent turned and left, his departure as abrupt and silent as his arrival. I stood frozen in my doorway. My mind raced with a flood of questions. What was this about? Why was I, a man who had fought so hard to eradicate child trafficking under the alias Paul Steel, now in the crosshairs of the FBI?

I had spent years operating undercover, working in tandem with top government officials across numerous countries. I was relieved that it was not a child trafficker who had infiltrated my covert world, but the burning question remained: what did the FBI want from me? The silence in my house was stifling, a stark contrast to the thoughts spiraling into chaos in my mind. As I closed the door and locked it behind me, one thing was certain: my undercover work had somehow landed on the Department of Justice's radar, and the situation didn't look promising.

After the shock of what had transpired began to wear off, I reached for my phone and dialed my attorney, hands still trembling. My voice wavered as I explained that I had been summoned to appear before an FBI Grand Jury, and was entirely in the dark about the reasons. I described the encounter with the agent, whose icy demeanor still sent chills down my spine, and how he revealed the details of my undercover alias.

My attorney assured me he would start calling immediately to uncover the truth. As I waited, each minute dragged on, filling me with growing anxiety. My mind raced through worst-case scenarios, and I could feel my heartbeat pounding in my throat. An hour passed, but it felt like an eternity, with every moment adding to my unease.

Finally, the phone rang, and I snatched it up to hear my attorney's voice. To my confusion, he was laughing. "What's so funny?" I demanded, frustration boiling over. "This is not a laughing matter!"

He quickly composed himself and explained that he had spoken directly with the special agent in charge of that FBI division. What he discovered turned my fear into a mixture of relief and lingering confusion as he unraveled the entire story.

My attorney began to explain the chilling reality behind the FBI's actions. The Federal Bureau of Investigation had recently apprehended a major target in Mexico, an infamous escaped convict known as King Fernando within the criminal underworld. This dangerous man had fled across the border and was now trafficking children in Tijuana. In a relentless pursuit to dismantle the network of criminals associated with him, the special agent in charge of this case discovered how he had been corresponding with an American named Paul Steel.

Acting swiftly, he obtained a search warrant and accessed the new suspect's Gmail account. What he found was an extensive archive of communications that seemed to link Paul Steel to numerous high-level trafficking rings across Mexico, Haiti, the Dominican Republic, and Thailand. The emails contained detailed discussions about meetings and specific locations where victims were being sold. Each message seemed to provide further evidence of Steel's deep involvement in the dark underworld of human trafficking.

Convinced he had stumbled across a high-profile figure in the trafficking world, he began the painstaking process of uncovering additional details about this dangerous offender. He systematically gathered intelligence, believing he was on the verge of exposing a key player in an extensive criminal network.

Little did he know that Paul Steel was actually an undercover operator working secretly with foundations and governments world-wide. These emails were part of Steel's efforts to gather intelligence and coordinate rescue operations. Steel's correspondences were created to infiltrate trafficking rings, identify key players, and ultimately dismantle the networks from within, making him a vital asset rather than the notorious criminal he appeared to be.

Earlier that year, one of my undercover missions led me and four other operators to the shadowy streets of Tijuana, Mexico. The Mexican federal police had identified a disturbing surge in child trafficking along the US/Mexico border, particularly in Mexicali and Tijuana. They needed our team to go undercover and trace the source. During this mission, we were introduced to the infamous King Fernando by a twenty-two-year-old prostitute who confided that she had been under his control for over a decade. The dangerous criminal, Fernando, knew me only as Paul Steel. He had no idea that my team was covertly working for the Mexican Federal police as we carefully pieced together the details of his operations.

My undercover persona was a masterpiece of deception, complete with fake phone numbers, addresses, a polished corporate website, social media profiles, and email addresses. I knew the trafficking rings could be alarmingly sophisticated, so I was obsessed with covering my tracks. Every detail had to be perfect; every login to my fabricated social media had to go through a VPN, ensuring there was no trace back to my real identity or location in the US. This was not just a precaution—it was absolutely necessary in order to protect me and my loved ones.

With all my safety measures in place, how did the FBI agent manage to unmask the true identity of Paul Steel? We had been relentlessly cautious, aware of some criminals' deep web hacking capabilities. Yet, my attorney revealed what he had learned from the special agent leading the case against Fernando. As they accessed Paul Steel's Gmail account and discovered my email exchanges with child traffickers worldwide, they were convinced they had found a dangerous criminal. Still, they could not identify the true nature of who I really was.

Despite all my caution in managing the profile, one particular email betrayed me. It was an email from a trafficker that I had forwarded from Paul Steel to Patt, a former CIA agent collaborating with ACTO, the first foundation I had worked with in Colombia. In that email, I updated him on many of our operations and asked for counsel and direction during a mission in Mexico. That single email was the thread the FBI agent pulled to unravel the truth about who Paul Steel was.

After uncovering my true identity, their focus shifted entirely to gathering information on King Fernando and any other details I had regarding the case. All the additional correspondence and intelligence collected were handed over. That night, sleep came easily, knowing my alias remained secure. Despite the close call, confidence in the cover remained strong, allowing the essential work in the shadows to continue—contributing to the fight against trafficking without compromising the safety of my family.

The only undercover operation I ever undertook as my true self, Paul Hutchinson, was that first mission on the island of Colombia. The unexpected phone call from Cassius gave me only two days to get on the ground with the traffickers. There was no time to fabricate an alias, and he wanted to use my real identity to convince the criminals that I had the resources to finance their resort. He presented images from my Facebook page, showcasing a luxury lifestyle, with photos of me on yachts and at exclusive events. The stakes were incredibly high.

Venturing into this mission without the protection of an alias was a considerable risk, but it was a risk I was willing to take to ensure the operation's success. Cassius believed that leveraging my true identity would lend authenticity to our cover story, making it more believable to the traffickers. The criminals needed to see me as a wealthy investor who could bankroll their illicit endeavors without hesitation. My genuine Facebook photos were powerful evidence of my supposed wealth and connections, convincing the traffickers that I was exactly who the pre-op team said I was.

14

IDENTITY ERASED

A Chance to Redefine Yourself

After the successful rescue mission in Colombia, the urge to share our life-changing stories with the world tugged at the consciences of me and the other operators. We wanted others to see the reality of child trafficking and experience the same emotional transformation we had. Cassius, however, strongly advised against public disclosure by any operators other than himself. He emphasized that if we chose to continue the role in rescue missions, it was imperative to maintain utmost secrecy. He said that any public exposure would jeopardize not only our safety but also the success of future operations. To achieve this, we had to retreat into a private sphere, deactivating most of our social media and adopting an alias for communication with traffickers.

Claiming credibility from his background as a former government agent, Cassius was adamant that he should become the face of the anti-child-trafficking cause. He would share video footage of Colombia's rescue and subsequent operations with the media. The remaining operators, including myself, would continue the covert work on the ground, orchestrating sting operations and rescuing children.

The strategy was to shield the identities of those directly involved in finding the traffickers while allowing Cassius to share the stories with the public. Recognizing the risks, we acknowledged the necessity of separating the visible storyteller from the undercover operatives. The public presence would serve as a powerful tool to shed light on the brutal reality of child trafficking. Television, radio, and documentaries became the mediums through which he narrated the riveting tales of our missions, detailing the rescued children's origins.

Unseen warriors, the true hidden heroes of the *Sound of Freedom*, continued their work. They included former Navy SEALs, Green Berets, Krav Maga trainers, ex-CIA agents, deep web hackers, and others without formal government training but driven by a commitment to liberating children from the grips of perpetrators.

To remain part of the undercover rescue missions, I was asked to make the difficult choice of relinquishing my public presence and stepping down from the board of directors of some of the charity organizations I was a part of. It was a monumental decision, as my public image and influential connections were deeply ingrained in my personal and professional life. The choice was clear; I would prioritize the rescue missions, even if it meant sacrificing my public profile.

Witnessing the horrors of child trafficking forever changed my perspective. The comfortable bubble of my affluent lifestyle became less appealing than the opportunity to contribute to bringing innocent children to safety. Driven by a sense of responsibility, I committed to closing down my social media, resigning from the charity boards, and removing my profile from my own company's website, all in the pursuit of freeing victims from the unspeakable horror of sex trafficking.

After making these difficult decisions to minimize my true public identity, the plan was for trained operators to go deep undercover to infiltrate the trafficking rings and set up sting operations. My role was to act as a wealthy playboy, funding the parties and being present during the rescue missions. My extravagant lifestyle and carefully crafted online image would provide a convincing backstory for the operators to share with the traffickers. This disguise would establish credibility and make it easier for the operators to gain the trust of the traffickers and gather important information.

By portraying a lavish life filled with yachts, beautiful women, and exotic cars, I would look like the perfect client to the traffickers, further embedding our team within their operations. This approach blended seamlessly with my real-life persona, making the cover story more believable and enhancing the success of the sting operations. The realistic depiction of wealth and luxury helped our team gain the traffickers' trust and gather essential intelligence without raising suspicion.

Understanding the apparent dangers of these situations, we knew creating a convincing fake profile was necessary. This new identity was essential for gaining the trust of traffickers as we infiltrated their networks. To protect myself and my loved ones, we had to remove any trace of my real identity from social media and other online platforms. This meant systematically eliminating any information linking my face to my home, children, family, and other personal details. Once the real Paul Hutchinson was erased from the internet, we needed to meticulously construct a fake online persona, ensuring it was credible enough to withstand scrutiny from the criminals we were targeting. This detailed approach was crucial for my safety and the success of our operations.

My executive assistant at the time, Kitty, was a remarkable woman. Brilliant and witty, she could type faster than I could think. During our conversations, I would ask her to send an email or look something up online, and she would already have it done before I could even finish explaining. Kitty was truly exceptional.

I told Kitty, "Here is what we need to do. First, we must remove anything related to the real me from the internet. Close down my personal Facebook, Instagram, and other social media pages. Remove my face from any boards of directors and anything else we can find online." It was a painstaking task. After she removed all traces of Paul Hutchinson, we needed to create a new undercover profile. Other operators would use this new profile to show traffickers and convince them to bring out all their victims to a party or other activity I was sponsoring.

I told her I still wanted to be called Paul, as it would be easier for everyone to remember while undercover. After all, over a million people are named Paul worldwide, making it unlikely that traffickers would connect that name to me. But I needed to change my last name and persona. So, I asked Kitty, "Can you set up an undercover profile? Create a brand-new fake profile for me under the name Paul Johnson." Kitty was typing away, capturing every detail of our conversation. Then she stopped, looked up at me, and said, "You have a chance to redefine yourself, and you are choosing Paul Johnson? Really? How about Paul Stone?

"She is brilliant!" I thought, "Paul Stone." Now, that sounds like the name of a secret agent or maybe even a rock star. It was perfect for the rich playboy image we needed to lure in the traffickers. We could craft a character that exuded confidence, wealth, and mystery with that name. It was precisely the bait we needed.

With the help of some friends in the web design business, we dove into creating this new identity from scratch. First, we set up a polished, professional-looking webpage with a portfolio showcasing Paul Stone's luxurious lifestyle and business ventures. We fabricated addresses, linking him to high-end properties around the world. Our goal was to build a convincing digital footprint so no one would question its authenticity.

Kitty was incredibly efficient, building social media profiles with hundreds of friends and followers, none of whom had any connection to the real me. We used a mix of my existing photos, fake interactions, and intricate backstories to give Paul Stone a vibrant, convincing online presence. Every detail was painstakingly crafted to ensure that Paul Stone seemed like a legitimate, wealthy businessman with a wild side.

We created connections to fictitious people and organizations, adding comments, likes, and shares to posts to simulate real engagement. We even linked Paul Stone's profiles to fake news articles and blogs that praised his business acumen and luxurious lifestyle. This level of detail was essential to fooling any traffickers who might try to dig deeper.

Paul Stone was no longer just an alias but a living, breathing entity in the digital world. This new identity was our gateway to infiltrating the darkest corners of the child trafficking networks, and we were ready to use it to its full potential.

This new alias, Paul Stone, founder of Paul Stone Capital, became the central figure for operators to lure in traffickers across Mexico and the Caribbean. Deep-cover pre-operation teams on the ground, from Acapulco to the Dominican Republic, used this new profile of a rich playboy who financed extravagant parties to attract traffickers and set up successful child rescue operations. However, this facade could not last forever.

To avoid raising suspicion, each sting operation concluded with federal agents arresting Paul Stone and his associates along with the traffickers, concealing my involvement in the sting. Yet, it was only a matter of time before the name and profile of Paul Stone spread to other parts of the trafficking networks, potentially compromising future operations.

After numerous undercover operations as Paul Stone, I was asked if I would be willing to take on a whole new level of infiltration. My next mission was to dive even deeper into the heart of the criminal underworld. Instead of posing as a wealthy, depraved buyer, I would join the pre-operation team tasked with identifying and locating human traffickers. This role would place me directly in the line of fire, face to face with some of the most dangerous people in the planet's seediest, most perilous cities.

This assignment demanded a complete transformation. My new identity had to withstand the scrutiny of hardened criminals and corrupt officials. The stakes were higher, the risks greater, and the dangers more immediate. We needed a new identity that could navigate these dangerous waters. Answering the call, Paul Steel was born.

Paul Steel was a different beast altogether. While Paul Stone was flashy and flamboyant, Paul Steel had to be tough, resourceful, and persistent. I needed to blend into the most dangerous environments without attracting unwanted attention. We crafted an identity that could seamlessly integrate into the criminal underworld, with a backstory rich in detail and shadowy enough to make the traffickers feel comfortable with me.

Our team of fearless operators adopted alias names like Andrew Westins, Jimmy Farley, Jaxon Wright, and Jeremy Hunt. These men are some of the best human beings I have ever had the privilege of knowing. They nobly placed themselves in harm's way to ensure the safety of the children. Their courage and dedication are unmatched, and they have shown incredible valor on numerous missions.

The incredible stories of these brave men and their heroic efforts will be detailed in future books of the Child Liberation Series. Each mission we undertook together demonstrated their unwavering commitment to justice and the protection of the innocent. Their actions have saved countless lives, and their legacy will continue to inspire and guide others in the fight against human trafficking.

Operating under the alias Paul Steel, Andrew and I navigated the gritty streets of downtown Port-au-Prince, Haiti, where the sanctity of life was often disregarded. Our mission expanded as Jimmy joined the team, and together, we braved the dangerous zones of Cancun, Tijuana, Cabo, and the Dominican Republic, infiltrating shadowy networks that thrived in these areas.

Jeremy brought an additional layer of security to our operations as we pursued leads from the infamous red-light district of Mexico City to orchestrate the largest child rescue in Mexico's history in Puerto Vallarta. Our work then took us from Ecuador's beaches to Bangkok's bustling streets, where human lives were traded like commodities. Each location presented unique dangers, requiring us to be constantly vigilant and prepared for anything.

Creating Paul Steel's online profile was an intricate process. We built a persona that could pass any test, with connections to criminal enterprises and a history that could fool even the most suspicious minds. Every piece of information was carefully curated to support the illusion, from social media interactions to business dealings.

This new identity was our shield and our weapon, allowing our team to gather essential intelligence and get close to the heart of the trafficking networks. It was a dangerous game, but we were ready. Paul Steel was ready. The mission was to infiltrate, gather intel, and bring down the traffickers from within their own networks.

15

God's Children are Not for Sale

Taken From the Church House Steps

The muffled scream of a child did not draw any attention to the families getting out of their religious service. It was on a beautiful Sunday morning just outside Port-au-Prince; the tranquil serenity around the old church house was shattered. A four-year-old boy, born in the United States, was taken in broad daylight in front of the Haitian church. His father, a devoted minister, had brought his family to Haiti with the goal of bringing light and hope to a troubled region. Little did he know, darkness was about to engulf his world.

The kidnappers were heartless criminals prowling in the darkness of the city. They thought the minister must have some money and decided to target him for ransom. With quick and ruthless precision, they kidnapped the child, leaving the father desperate and frantic.

The traffickers demanded money, and the father paid the ransom without hesitation, praying for his son's safe return. However, his hope faded when a second, larger demand came. He did not have the kind of money they wanted. His message to the traffickers explaining that he could not pay would be the last communication the distressed father had with the criminals.

Knowing they could make additional cash from the little boy in other ways, the traffickers vanished, taking the child with them into the heart of the unknown, leaving a trail of anguish and fear behind. The father's world fell into darkness, his faith tested as he realized the horror of his son's situation.

Dave Lopez, a former Navy SEAL who commanded the team in Medellin, Colombia, spearheaded a series of undercover operations in Haiti, driven by his determination to help the minister find his kidnapped child. During the first mission, 28 children were rescued, but the child was not among them. When the father received the news that his son was not one of those saved, his heart sank, and a deep sorrow washed over him. For a moment, he bowed his head, the weight of grief pressing down on his shoulders, knowing his beloved son was still missing. Yet, with a strength that gives hope to humanity, he lifted his head and forced a smile through the pain.

"Because my son was taken," he said, his voice trembling but firm, "you came to find him, and now 28 children are safe, rescued from the unspeakable horrors of trafficking. If losing my son means these children can be free, it is a burden I am willing to accept."

The team's involvement in Haiti began with a mission to locate and rescue this child because he was an American. But as we went deeper into the heart-wrenching reality of the situation, it did not matter what nationality the children were. No child should be for sale regardless of where they come from. Every child across the globe of every religion, ethnicity, and skin color deserves freedom from the chains of slavery. This commitment has carried me and our teams to all corners of the earth.

As we proclaimed in the *Sound of Freedom* movie,
"God's children are not for sale!"

Today, hundreds of human trafficking victims in Haiti have been rescued while searching for that one little boy taken from the church. But this victory is bittersweet. For every life saved, thousands more are still trapped in the nightmare of modern slavery. It often feels like fighting an endless battle, with each rescue showing us even more darkness and reminding us how many more are still suffering.

During one particular mission, it was discovered that the child trafficking ring was functioning as an operation involving organ harvesting. This encounter was both shocking and deeply disturbing. To ensure we were prepared for any emergencies, a military trauma doctor accompanied us, ready to address any severe injuries that might arise during the mission.

Perplexed and sickened by the thought of this kind of operation, I could not help but question the doctor about the demand for organs harvested from children. I asked him who could be so desperate or morally bankrupt as to pay for such organs, fully aware of their horrendous and inhumane origins. The thought of such a market existing was horrifying and emphasized the dark reality we were up against.

The doctor shared a startling statistic that left me in disbelief: approximately 10 percent of all organ transplants involve trafficked organs. He explained that human traffickers often exploit their victims in the sex trade until they are no longer sellable, after which they make one final, wicked transaction by selling their organs on the black market. Around 10,000 kidneys are illegally traded each year globally, translating to more than one kidney being sold every hour. The scale of the problem can seem overwhelming, but every rescue strengthens our resolve to keep fighting and bring hope to the darkest corners of this crisis.

The deeper we went undercover in Haiti, the more we realized the true extent of the problem. The country's severe poverty, combined with some of the worst political corruption in the world, makes it a breeding ground for the worst aspects of humanity. Every day, we encountered heartbreaking stories of families torn apart, children sold into slavery, and communities living in fear. The lack of economic opportunities drives many to desperation, making them easy targets for traffickers who exploit their vulnerability.

Haiti's crumbling infrastructure and limited access to education, healthcare, and essential services exacerbate the situation. The political landscape is rife with corruption, with officials often ignoring the suffering or, worse, being complicit in these crimes. This widespread corruption allows traffickers to operate freely, knowing they are unlikely to face justice.

The scale of human trafficking in Haiti is staggering. Children are kidnapped or sold by their impoverished families, promised a better life, only to be subjected to unimaginable horrors. Women and young girls are forced into prostitution, while men and boys are coerced into brutal labor. The problem is both local and international, with victims trafficked across borders, making it a complex issue to tackle.

We found hope in a remarkable man named Jim in this overwhelming darkness. A native of Haiti, Jim became one of my most loyal friends and a source of inspiration. For most of his adult life, he tirelessly fought to help the Haitian people, displaying fearless strength in the face of adversity. His deep love and unwavering dedication to his country shone through in everything he did.

Jim worked in law enforcement, using his position to protect and serve his community. His commitment to justice and the well-being of others led him to become the lead operator on our undercover missions to fight child trafficking in Haiti. Jim's bravery and leadership were unmatched; he risked his life daily to rescue innocent children from trafficking. His selflessness and courage were not just professional traits but deeply personal values.

I first met Jim while accompanying a well-known TV and radio influencer to Haiti. The influencer wanted to film some of the rescued children in Haiti's orphanages and safe houses to showcase the positive work being done. During our visit, I was asked to join teams of operators on the ground to help identify additional trafficking rings. Despite the tireless efforts of countless charity foundations, trafficking in Haiti remained widespread.

Jim stood out immediately. His deep commitment to justice and his community was evident in every action. He had taken on the dangerous role of leading undercover missions to combat child trafficking. His bravery and leadership were unmatched, as he risked his life daily to rescue innocent children from horrific conditions.

Our mission was to disrupt the criminal network at its core and make a lasting impact on the region. Jim's expertise and experience were essential in identifying and dismantling trafficking networks. His unwavering dedication and passion for fighting corruption inspired everyone around him. Working alongside Jim and his team, we aimed not only to rescue the children but also to deliver a significant blow to the trafficking operations that plagued Haiti.

Almost three years had passed since the Cartagena, Colombia rescue mission, and now I found myself in the dark alleys of Port-au-Prince, Haiti. In those years, I had participated in over 30 covert missions worldwide. My role had changed dramatically; I went from posing as a wealthy buyer of children to conducting deep cover operations. We worked closely with federal agents, venturing into the night to uncover the darkest parts of humanity. I had served with an elite team of operators on the streets, exposing the worst criminals involved in child trafficking. Our mission had become more dangerous, but we were more determined than ever to bring these predators to justice.

Starting at the bottom, we built trust with the drug dealers and pimps on the streets, each interaction bringing us one step closer to the people truly in control. To make a real impact on fighting trafficking and have any chance of finding the little boy taken from the church, we needed to stay deeply embedded in Haiti's underworld until we could identify and destroy the central hierarchy exploiting children in the region.

16

THE RED DOOR

I Did not Think Anyone Would Come

S
tanding at 6'4" and nearly 300 pounds of solid muscle, Aaron was an intimidating man, a powerful force for good in the dark world of child trafficking. We found ourselves in a dangerous situation, cornered by child traffickers following behind us and a rundown truck obstructing our only escape route from one of the most dangerous neighborhoods in Port-au-Prince, Haiti. The tension was high, and our lives were at stake. Without a moment's hesitation, Aaron sprang from our vehicle, his sheer presence enough to send a shiver down anyone's spine. With a thunderous roar, he harnessed every ounce of his strength, gripping the truck's chassis and hoisting it with a Herculean effort. Aaron's determination was unstoppable as he heaved the truck aside, creating a path for our desperate escape, his act of raw power and bravery searing itself into our memories forever.

This fearless man hails from an extraordinary family of warriors and is the brother of one of our elite undercover operators, Andrew McCubbins, known by the alias Andrew Westins. Years earlier, upon learning about the Colombian child rescue mission, Andrew joined our team and quickly became a vital asset. He was among the initial investors in the script for the *Sound of Freedom* movie and directly participated in some of the missions portrayed in the film. Andrew and I had worked together on undercover operations all over the globe. Andrew had persuaded his brother Aaron to join us for this mission in Haiti, providing additional security for one of the most perilous undercover child rescue missions we had ever encountered. Port-au-Prince has a reputation for being one of the world's most volatile and dangerous cities. Violent crimes, including murder, armed robbery, kidnapping, assault, and carjacking, are rampant. Criminal gangs dominate many regions, and even humanitarian aid workers are often viewed as legitimate targets.

The extensive political corruption, gang violence, drug trafficking, and organized crime demanded constant attentiveness. We had to stay alert to ensure our safety as we infiltrated the country's largest trafficking organizations. The stakes were incredibly high, but our mission was unwavering: to dismantle the insidious trafficking rings in the Caribbean, fueled by widespread corruption.

Andrew and I had traveled back and forth from the US many times, spending over three months deep undercover in Haiti to gain the trust of criminals in the Caribbean's most notorious trafficking rings. Each operation was fraught with danger as we carefully climbed the ranks, aiming to connect with level 3 traffickers, those who physically held the children ready for sale. It took countless face-to-face meetings and eight high-stakes missions to penetrate the inner circles and reach the elusive kingpin of Port-au-Prince.

This boss, a heartless female trafficker named Cho, had been a legend in the criminal underworld for decades. Cho was a large, heavy-set woman with an iron grip on the dark trade, known for her ruthless efficiency in selling children. Her presence alone inspired fear and obedience, and her gang of brutal men protected her at all costs.

Andrew, Aaron, and I were leaving Cho's base of operations when the truck blocked our escape route. We had gained enough trust with her henchmen, and she agreed to show us places where she kept the children. After geotagging the location of her base, we knew it was time to make our exit. The federal agents backing our mission were nowhere near this risky neighborhood, ruled by dangerous criminals, and we were on our own.

We had carefully navigated the maze-like streets of this part of Haiti, an area so dangerous that even the police avoided it. Aaron's brute strength in moving the truck may have saved our lives that day. Most importantly, we now had clear evidence that Cho was operating one of the most extensive child trafficking rings in Port-au-Prince, which included children taken from the Dominican Republic and even the sale of her own daughter.

Our mission was to cut the head off the dragon: dismantle the monstrous network of human trafficking in the Caribbean by taking down the top criminals orchestrating these heinous acts. After months of painstaking undercover work, our efforts were beginning to show results. We had identified multiple child trafficking rings, each responsible for the exploitation of hundreds of innocent victims. The top-tier traffickers we uncovered were a chilling mix of society's worst—drug dealers, strip club owners, and, shockingly, even federal judges.

Navigating through the raw sewage of criminals who preyed on children was a stomach-turning endeavor, but it was a necessary journey to get to the top. We needed to trace the connections, follow the money, and expose the kingpins pulling the strings behind this vile enterprise. Our resolve was fueled by the faces of the victims we sought to save, knowing that our efforts could bring justice and end their suffering.

A few weeks earlier, Cho had agreed to show us a covert location in the city where she was keeping the children. This evil lair, where the unthinkable happened, lay in the heart of a dark and dangerous part of town notorious for its drug dealers and prostitutes. The air seemed thick with danger as Andrew and I followed her men deeper into the heart of Port-au-Prince, Haiti, through dark alleyways, our awareness sharpening with every step.

Eventually, we arrived at an imposing steel door painted a blood red. It stood nearly four feet wide and seven feet tall, a grim sentinel guarding the horrors within. Cho scanned the streets for unwelcome observers as she carefully inserted a key into the heavy lock, the metallic click breaking the silence of the ominous night. The door creaked open to reveal a narrow, dirty hallway, its dim lighting casting eerie shadows on the walls.

We proceeded down the hallway, our senses heightened by the oppressive darkness and the stench of decay. A series of cell doors lined the corridor to our left, each a wretched testament to the suffering hidden behind them. Cho paused at one of these doors, her movements deliberate and slow as she selected another key. The lock turned with a reluctant prod, and the door swung open.

What we saw inside made our stomachs churn, and our hearts ache. The room was no more than six feet deep and scarcely a few feet wide, a claustrophobic cell that reeked of neglect and misery. A steel plank, bolted to the wall and held up by a rusted chain, served as a crude bed. A filthy, tattered blanket, riddled with holes, lay atop the plank, offering meager comfort to its small occupant. The sight was enough to break even the hardest of hearts.

Then, I saw something that made my blood run cold. To the left of the steel plank, a small girl sat on a concrete block on the floor. Her bare feet rested in the dirt, her tiny frame hunched over in defeat. The blank, sorrowful expression on her face spoke volumes of the torment she had endured. Her eyes were empty of all emotion as she looked up at me, a hollow gaze piercing my soul. At that moment, she saw me as just another man who had come to abuse her, another monster in a long line of tormentors. Little did she know, this was the beginning of her long-awaited liberation.

This child was just fourteen years old. She had been ripped from the safety of her family at the tender age of seven, her innocence stolen in the aftermath of the Haiti earthquake. Her parents, victims of that horrible tragedy, had left her orphaned and vulnerable. For seven long years, she had been sold like a commodity, forced to endure unimaginable horrors up to twenty times a day. The life she had known was a relentless cycle of pain and suffering; the cruelty of human trafficking destroyed her childhood.

As I stood there, a wave of anger and sorrow washed over me. The weight of her suffering hung heavy in the air, the reality of her plight crashing down on me like a tidal wave. This young girl, stripped of her innocence and hope, had survived pain that no child should ever face. The sight of her, broken and weary, fueled my burning determination. This was not just another mission but an opportunity to pull this child out of Hell and bring a glimmer of hope to a life filled with darkness. The road to her liberation had begun, and nothing would stand in our way. Andrew and I would remain steadfast as her protectors, putting our very lives in danger for the freedom of the children in that compound.

That little girl did not utter a single word for two weeks after we rescued her. The trauma she had endured left her unable and unwilling to speak, her eyes filled with an emptiness that spoke of years of suffering. When she finally broke her silence, the words she spoke brought everyone to tears:

"I did not think anyone would come."

The weight of her simple statement was overwhelming. This young girl, barely more than a child, had given up hope long ago, resigned to a life of unending torment. The fury that rushed through me was ignited by the realization that every man who had passed through those doors before us had only come to inflict pain, to prolong her torment. Andrew and I were the first to enter with the purpose of rescuing her, of bringing a glimmer of hope.

The injustice of it all filled me with a burning rage. How could the world allow such cruelty to exist? How could so many perpetrators disregard the agony of this innocent child? She had been trapped in a nightmare, her every day filled with fear and pain, believing no one would ever come to her rescue.

Now, due to the bravery of many operators, she is safe, surrounded by extended family members who shower her with the love and care she had been so cruelly denied. She is learning to dance, her once rigid body beginning to move with the tentative grace of a child rediscovering joy. Reclaiming her lost childhood, she is going to school, her mind awakening to the possibilities of a future that had once seemed impossible. Every small victory, every step she takes towards building back her fractured life, is a witness to the strength of the human spirit.

17

EXPOSED AND IMPRISONED

Judgment Day in Haiti – Superbowl Sunday

Boom! The door of the small beachside villa blasted open, shattering the quiet negotiations between our team and the traffickers. Chaos erupted instantly as federal agents stormed in. "On the ground! Everyone on the ground!" they shouted, their commands emphasized by the sight of their weapons, a clear warning of their deadly determination.

The room filled with foreign agents, a wave of relentless force, shoving us to the ground with callous hands. The cold, gritty floor met my cheek as I was pinned down, my heart pounding in my chest. I was held on the ground between two traffickers, their eyes wide with panic, the federal agent placing his knee on my back as he bound my hands, a chilling reminder of the danger of this mission.

It was Super Bowl Sunday. Instead of the roar of the crowd and the thrill of the game, I was in Haiti, on the ground among nine of the worst kinds of people on the planet. The adrenaline surged through me, a twisted sense of excitement mingling with the danger—my kind of party.

A Haitian federal agent, unaware that I was one of the good guys, roughly patted me down. His hand paused as he felt the hidden inner pocket in my pants. My heart sank as he pulled out my American passport. His eyes narrowed as he read my name, a look of suspicion crossing his face. Without a word, he placed it atop the growing pile of gathered evidence from the traffickers.

Panic rushed through me.
This is bad. This is very, very bad...

At this moment, lying on the ground with a Haitian federal officer binding my wrists, our undercover team was supposed to be "arrested" with the traffickers. This facade was essential to maintain our cover and ensure a safe exit from the country. The traffickers needed to believe that we were being taken into custody and then potentially extradited to the US to stand trial. The plan was simple: traffickers would be taken to prison, while my fellow operatives and I would be escorted to the airport for a quick and safe exit from the country. The only time I had my real identity on my person during an operation was on the day of the sting to ensure I could get through security at the airport once we arrived.

Operating under the alias "Paul Steel," I had carefully created this identity to work undercover without the risk of traffickers discovering my true identity. This false profile protected me from revenge, ensuring that even when these criminals were imprisoned, they could not send their associates after me.

Due to the large number of traffickers being apprehended during this sting operation, the Haitian federal police ran out of handcuffs. The agent binding me resorted to using very thick zip ties behind my back. Unaware that I was actually one of the good guys, he pulled them exceedingly tight, cutting off the blood flow to my hands.

As he lifted me off the floor and escorted me outside toward the awaiting police car, I suddenly felt a sharp pain in my side. Someone had thrown a rock at me! Then, a barrage of stones and gravel began coming from all directions. The locals had discovered the party exploiting trafficked children, and their anger was intense. They were now throwing things at me and my operator, who was also bound with zip ties. Constrained and defenseless, we could do nothing as the officers shielded our heads with their hands, quickly rushing us to the squad car amid the chaos.

Finally, inside the safety of the police car, I looked up and saw a familiar face—it was Jim. A sense of peace washed over me as I recognized one of the few people in Haiti I truly trusted. Jim knew I was on the right side of this fight, and his presence was a lifeline amid the confusion. I breathed a sigh of relief, knowing that he would take us to the safety of the awaiting plane. At that moment, surrounded by hostility and danger, the sight of Jim brought a wave of reassurance and hope. He gave me a quick nod, his eyes filled with understanding and determination, and I knew we would make it out safely.

Bang! Bang! Bang! My temporary relief was shattered. I turned suddenly to see a large man outside the car holding a stick. The furious crowd was battering the police car, their anger erupting. The operator sitting next to me had not experienced this level of chaos on a mission, and a cold sweat broke out on his forehead. There was no time for chit-chat with Jim; we needed to get out of there now.

Jim hit the gas; his eyes locked with determination on the path forward as he navigated around parked cars and the mob, pushing through the panic that threatened to overwhelm my comrade. The vehicle jolted and swerved, each bump heightening his anxiety. Finally, we reached the exit and sped away from the threatening crowd. As the resort receded into the distance, we all felt a surge of gratitude and relief wash over us, knowing we had narrowly escaped the danger.

Jim calmly pulled the police car to the side of the road. Turning around, he held up some handcuff keys, smiled, and said, "Are you ready to get out of those shackles?"

"We are both zip-tied," I exclaimed. "Do you have a pair of pliers or a knife?"

"No," Jim responded, his smile fading. "I do not have anything like that on me. We must wait for another officer or get something from a store to cut you free."

A serious look came over my face. "We have a bigger problem," I said, my voice carrying a tone of concern. One of the officers took my passport and placed it with the evidence from the traffickers."

Jim's eyes widened. "We can't go back there!" he exclaimed. "That place is a war zone!"

I nodded, feeling the weight of our situation. "We will have to wait until the evidence arrives at the police station to retrieve it."

The car was silent for a moment, the seriousness of our situation sinking in. The angry mob was behind us, but we were far from safe. Jim and I exchanged a glance, a silent understanding passing between us. We were in this together, and somehow, we would find a way out.

After an excruciating drive with painfully tight zip ties, we finally managed to get them cut off. Then, we waited at the federal police headquarters to retrieve my passport along with the evidence from the traffickers. Finally retrieving it, we were escorted to the airport, where a Gulfstream jet patiently awaited our departure.

One of the world's top influencers and personal coaches was on the jet. He had flown in to witness the takedown of the most notorious trafficking rings in Haiti and the rescue of dozens of children. As I stepped onto the plane, the influencer stood up. He was massive at 6'7" and had a heart equally as massive. His gigantic hands came together, initiating an applause that quickly spread throughout the cabin.

The recognition was incredibly heartwarming, a rare moment of appreciation in the shadows of undercover work. I had spent four long, grueling months fighting my way to the top kingpins in Haiti. The nights were filled with danger, the days with relentless pursuit. My body ached from the constant strain, and my mind was weary from the endless deception. Yet, as the clapping filled the plane, the weight of those months seemed to lift, replaced by a deep feeling sense of accomplishment.

The applause was not just for me but for every child we had saved, every life we had touched, and every operator who selflessly served to help rescue them. The hard work had paid off, resulting in one of the Caribbean's most successful child rescue missions ever.

Tears welled up in my eyes as I looked around at the smiling faces, the genuine gratitude and admiration. It was a moment I would never forget, a reminder of why we do what we do. The influencer, towering above the rest, continued to clap, his eyes shining with emotion. His presence and acknowledgment were powerful, making all the sacrifices feel worthwhile.

Two weeks later, we received shocking news: the traffickers we had just arrested had bribed four corrupt judges in Haiti with $80,000 USD to allow their release from prison. To put this in perspective, Haiti's annual income per capita at that time was about $1,400. This means $80,000 is equivalent to fifty-seven times the yearly income in Haiti. Based on the average income there versus the US, this would be like paying nearly $4.5 million in bribes in the United States. The extensive corruption was our biggest challenge in Haiti.

The traffickers were now back on the streets, resuming their dreadful business of trafficking victims. Freed from the legal constraints that had briefly halted their operations, they wasted no time in returning to their cruel and abusive activities. Vulnerable children once again found themselves at risk as these criminals looked for new targets.

Besides months of undercover work going down the drain, the issue for me was the federal judges' justification for releasing the traffickers. They claimed that the real criminals were the Americans who had escaped. What I had not realized when we picked up my passport at the police station was that it had already been logged into the system as evidence, not under any of my undercover aliases like Paul Stone, Paul Steel, or Paul Black, but under my real name: Paul Hutchinson.

As I grasped the terrifying truth, I realized the seriousness of my situation. My real identity was exposed in a corrupt system, making me a target. The crooked judges turned my undercover work into an even more dangerous game. The stakes were higher than ever, putting the mission and my life at risk. Instantly, I knew the potential danger of retaliation. I could never set foot in Haiti again without looking over my shoulder. I was now a marked man in one of the world's most dangerous and corrupt countries.

Jim escorted the First Lady of Haiti and several Haitian diplomats to the US for a full briefing on our operation and how they could help address the situation. It would have been too dangerous to have such a meeting in Haiti, not to mention the risk it would pose to blowing my cover. We laid out all the evidence—every photo, every text from the traffickers. Jim's deep love for his native Haiti was clear, and the anger in his eyes was unmistakable as he turned to me and said, "I don't care if I lose my job. I don't care if I lose my life. I am going to clean up the corruption in my country!"

18

INTO THE HORNET'S NEST

A Battle Against Federal Corruption

J im and the team flew back to Haiti with former Navy SEAL Dave
Lopez and ripped open the hornet's nest. Leading the charge,
they targeted the corrupt federal judges and re-arrested the
traffickers, determined to bring justice and safety to Jim's homeland.
Their unwavering dedication ignited a spark of hope in all of us,
inspiring a renewed fight against the corruption that plagued Haiti.

This operation had unleashed the wrath of Satan himself, the
ultimate adversary of all that is good. Instantly, civil unrest in
Port-au-Prince escalated. The battle between good and evil intensified, reaching a fever pitch. Tires burned in the streets, political
assassinations became routine, and the country plunged deeper into
chaos. This turmoil revealed the monstrous corruption tied to child
trafficking in the region. As federal judges were exposed and billions
of dollars in missing humanitarian aid came to light, the shocking
extent of the exploitation became undeniable.

As Jim sought ways to alleviate the suffering of children in Haiti,
one of his primary concerns was the Restavek program, which contributes to trafficking and child exploitation. "Restavek" describes
a heartbreaking reality where a child is given away by their parents
to become a domestic servant because the family can't provide for
them. These vulnerable children are sometimes sent from their rural

homes to live with wealthier or less impoverished people in urban areas. Although the intention might be to offer them food, shelter, and occasionally an education in exchange for their labor, the reality is often much harsher.

Many restaveks are forced into exploitation with little to no access to education. Instead of receiving care and opportunities, they are frequently subjected to physical, emotional, and sexual abuse. These children live in constant fear, performing grueling tasks for their host families without any rights or protections. Their plight is often ignored by authorities, making it easy for traffickers to take advantage of their already desperate situations.

This disturbing practice reflects the darkest aspects of modern-day slavery and child trafficking, with an estimated 300,000 Haitian children trapped in such conditions, deprived of education while also subjected to excessive labor. Alarmingly, 25 percent of Haitian children aged 5–17 are separated from their biological parents, leading lives filled with hardship and despair.

Jim explained that drug cartels in the region often force restavek children to work on their jungle-based drug-growing operations, which might be part of our next mission. He explained how there was evidence suggesting that the American boy taken from the church might be in a dangerous jungle area between Haiti and the Dominican Republic. This region is extremely remote; the nearest police station is over 10 hours away, requiring five hours of driving on treacherous dirt roads and another five hours of hiking or horse-back riding through the jungle.

While Andrew, Jimmy, Joseph, and I were undercover in Tijuana, Mexico, fighting trafficking near the US border, a team of former Special Forces operators was dispatched to Haiti to follow up on the intel about the boy. As they drove toward the jungle, they encoun-tered immediate hostility from the locals, who were armed with pitchforks and shotguns. The locals made it clear that outsiders were not welcome, surrounding the vehicles with anger and suspicion. Recognizing the severe risk, the team decided to abort the mission, understanding that continuing into the cartel-controlled jungle without a better plan would be suicidal.

Sending Navy SEALs into a remote jungle area would inevitably draw unwanted attention. To infiltrate the area effectively, a more covert approach was necessary. After careful consideration, the decision was made to send a small team posing as doctors. This way, they could earn the trust of the locals and gather important information without making anyone suspicious.

The idea of posing as a doctor while undercover is not new. Many operators have successfully used this disguise for various missions over the years. In fact, at the time of this operation, the script for *Sound of Freedom* was already written with the doctor scene and based on numerous missions and the experiences of hundreds of operators.

The reason the disguise is so effective is the fact that over 85 percent of survivors are reported to have had contact with a healthcare professional while being trafficked. Keeping the victims somewhat healthy is vital for the financial stability of trafficking organizations, so they are willing to risk taking them for medical care. Unfortunately, many healthcare professionals do not realize their patients are trafficking victims, so these cases often go unreported.

Upon returning from undercover work in Mexico, I received an urgent phone call from Jim in Haiti. "We need you back." He went on to explain, "The mission with the Navy SEALs was not successful. They looked too intimidating to infiltrate that region. You are effective in your undercover work because you do not appear threatening to the traffickers. You could pass as a doctor and get into that jungle area."

His words weighed heavily on me. With its inescapable corruption and a target on my back, the thought of returning to Haiti was concerning. However, Jim's plea made it clear how critical the situation was. The traffickers needed to be stopped, and innocent lives were at stake. Despite our reservations, we knew we had to go back. My ability to blend in and gain the trust of those in the underworld was a unique advantage we could not afford to lose. Jim believed in me, and that belief fueled my resolve. The mission was dangerous, but the chance to make a difference and rescue more children outweighed my concerns.

With a hint of humor, I told Jim, "You know I was '*Haiti's Most Wanted*' just a few months ago, right?" I was referring to the corrupt judges who had framed me to let the traffickers walk free.

"Yes," Jim replied, "but now you will be Haiti's most protected."

"That does not exactly fill me with confidence!" I exclaimed, my voice filled with a mix of excitement and legitimate concern. "The corruption runs so deep that you are the only person I trust."

"I will be with you every step of the way," Jim assured me, his voice steady. "These guys won't get to you!"

Jim outlined a two-phase plan to infiltrate the jungle area. The first phase aimed to establish credibility and goodwill in the region, while the second phase would involve a more intense operation deep into the jungle.

Phase one of the plan involved bringing twenty medical personnel from Port-au-Prince to a region the former Special Forces team couldn't reach. The goal was to make the clinic a major public event, ensuring that news of it spread quickly into the jungle. By presenting ourselves as doctors running the clinic, we aimed to build relationships with the locals. This way, word of our presence and activities would spread, making it easier for us to venture deeper into the jungle during phase two. The medical teams would serve as our cover, allowing us to enter the area discreetly.

The clinic's story and our role as doctors were key to gaining the locals' trust, which was essential for the success of phase two. The first phase, set in a relatively populated area on the jungle's outskirts, was ideal for building rapport with the community and was less dangerous. Because of this, Jim mentioned that Cassius would likely come to film the healthcare clinic as a publicity tactic.

With the trust and positive reputation established in phase one, phase two would take us deeper into the jungle. This phase would be more intense, but our groundwork would make it easier to navigate the region. Throughout both phases, we would continue to search for information on missing children, including the American boy.

"Do you think it is safe for me to fly into Port-au-Prince after everything that has happened with the corrupt judges?" I asked

Jim's response was immediate, his tone filled with concern. "I am not just worried about your safety in the city. Our entire team's security on the roads to the clinic site is at risk. The locals are still furious with the Special Forces group that tried to enter a few weeks ago. We need to find a safer route to the clinic."

I paused, considering our options. "What if we entered the region from the Dominican Republic side instead?" I suggested.

"That is a great idea!" Jim exclaimed. "Much safer than driving from Port-au-Prince."

I opened Google Earth and examined the clinic's location. I found several dirt roads leading to it from the Dominican Republic. Because of the recent corruption issues, this route seemed much safer. Feeling more at ease about avoiding Port-au-Prince, I agreed to take on the undercover role of a doctor for the mission.

This assignment touched on a childhood dream of mine—I had always wanted to be a doctor. Though my life had taken a different path, the desire to heal and help others never left me. Over the years, my work in child rescue earned me honorary doctorates, but I knew these were far different from a real MD. The distinction was clear, especially given the skills needed for this mission.

In this operation, the abilities we needed weren't those taught in pre-med classes or through years of academic study. Instead, we had to rely on the skills honed through years of undercover work and life-threatening missions. We had to be persuasive, convincing the villagers and traffickers alike that we were legitimate medical doctors. Our cover story had to be flawless to ensure everyone's safety and the mission's success.

This job required a unique blend of undercover expertise and a convincing medical façade. We had to merge our knowledge of child rescue with the role of a healthcare professional. The mission's success—and the children's lives—depended on our ability to master both roles.

19

ILLICIT BORDER CROSSING

The Search for a Lost Child

"An illegal border crossing? That will cost you six thousand dollars," said the man on the other line. Jim hung up the phone, his expression filled with worry. "This may be our only option," he said, his voice heavy with resignation. We had to cross that border within the next few hours, or we would miss the entire operation.

Despite our careful planning, the fight for freedom always encounters obstacles. My team had flown into Santo Domingo, Dominican Republic, rented a mid-sized SUV, and traveled the 150-mile journey toward the Haiti border. As we neared the border crossing, we realized our rental car could not handle the rough roads leading to the health clinic's remote location.

The timing was critical. We needed to arrive at the same time as the Haitian medical team to build credibility with the locals and ensure our safe passage deeper into the jungle for the next phase of our mission.

A young man rode up to us on an off-road motorcycle. "You will never make it in a car," he said. "The only way through these roads is on a dirt bike."

We explained to him that we were setting up a healthcare clinic in the area. He promised to spread the word to the men living in the jungle region and encourage them to bring their children for a checkup. He then urged us to follow him to a town where we could rent motorcycles.

Feeling optimistic, we followed the young man to the nearest town to see if we could rent suitable bikes.

"To go across the border?" the motorcycle shop owner exclaimed. "I will never see the bikes again. I won't rent them, but you can buy them for $2,000 cash each." These were old, run-down motorcycles, and we knew we were being taken advantage of, but the mission was extremely important. Everything else was in place. The real doctors and medical personnel from Haiti had already begun the five-hour drive from Port-au-Prince, and we needed to be there when they arrived.

I did not have enough cash to buy the motorcycles, so we found an ATM and began withdrawing the maximum amount each time. The machine would only dispense $60 per transaction, so it would take 100 separate cash retrievals to gather enough for the transaction. Each withdrawal felt like a small victory, but the pressure was mounting.

After 30 separate ATM transactions, Jim received a call from his inside connections in the government. "They have closed the border because of all the violence and unrest in Haiti," the general disclosed. The civil unrest in Haiti had continued to spike since Jim and the team took down the corrupt federal judges. It was a destabilization effort designed by the kingpins of trafficking in the country. Tires burning in the streets were just the tip of the iceberg as the iron grip of corruption realized it could be losing its hold on the region.

My mind raced. We had come too far to be stopped at the last minute! Considering every conceivable possibility, I racked my brain. "There has to be a way!" I exclaimed. Every decision, every dollar, and every moment counted as we fought against time and chaos to reach our goal.

"What about a helicopter?" I suggested. "Our options are running out; it might be the only way to make it in time for the clinic."

Jim shook his head. "Without proper paperwork, the pilot can't legally land on the Haitian side of the border. And with the border closure, we can't get authorization to fly from the DR to Haiti without getting approval days in advance."

"What if he flew a 'sightseeing' tour over the area we need to be, flew the helicopter low, and allowed us to jump out?" I suggested, grasping at straws. "I am already considered a felon in Haiti, so why not add to the list of offenses!"

Jim thought for a moment. "That will take a special type of pilot willing to bend the law a little. But I think I know just the guy."

With renewed hope, Jim called a trusted helicopter pilot in the area. After a tense conversation, Jim hung up and conveyed the pilot's message. "He'll do it, but it will cost $6,000 USD. The pilot said he could lose his license and even be imprisoned for a stunt like that, but this operation is essential."

We exchanged determined glances. The mission's importance outweighed the cost and the risks. Every second mattered as we scrambled to gather the funds and finalize the new plan. The clock was ticking, and the lives of many hung in the balance as we prepared for what could be the riskiest leg of our journey yet.

The pilot filed a flight plan to leave one Dominican city and fly to another Dominican city with a low-flying sightseeing trip over the border in Haiti. It was at least a two-hour drive to the airport, and we needed to be there in 45 minutes to make the fast-closing window of opportunity.

"What is the speed limit on this road?" asked Sean, my close friend and security detail for this operation. "There is no way we will make it on time at this rate."

"Do not worry about the speed," Jim responded. "You just make sure we reach the airport in the designated window. If we get stopped by the police, I will handle it."

In addition to his extensive combat and security training, Sean had raced the Baja 1,000, often called "the most dangerous race in the world." Deaths during the race are not uncommon, and the brutal Baja Mexico terrain sees only half of the teams reach the finish line. Sean's nerves of steel and unparalleled driving skills got him to the finish line once before, and now, those same skills would be tested again as he navigated the treacherous landscape to reach the helicopter in time.

Thanks to Sean's excellent driving skills, we arrived at the airport with time to spare. The helicopter had not yet arrived; Sean managed to beat the pilot to the airport. When the aircraft finally landed, we quickly jumped inside. Jim told the pilot we would pay half upfront and the other half once we landed safely back at the airport after the mission.

"How will you contact me once you are ready for extraction?" the pilot asked.

I pulled out my Iridium satellite phone. "Whenever I travel worldwide, there are always three things in my backpack: a water filtration straw, enough cash to return home in an emergency, and a satellite phone."

For this mission, we would need two of the three: the spare cash to cover the excessive flight fees and the satellite phone to arrange our pickup.

We took off and headed across the forbidden border. As we neared the predetermined site, the pilot let us out. Dressed in blue scrubs, we looked the part of kind doctors managing the clinic. The real work began: building relationships with the locals, carefully studying the faces of the children present, and trying to identify the little boy taken from the church years before.

We will refer to this child as Galli, the reason some of our operators first began doing rescue missions in Haiti. Galli was only four years old when he was taken. Years later, hundreds of children were liberated in Haiti because operators were searching for him.

Over 1,500 people came to the clinic, including about 200 adults and 1,300 children. The ratio of children to adults was suspiciously high. Many children were likely brought in through the Restavek program to help work in the fields. With so many children in the area, it was difficult to determine which ones were trafficked, which were part of the Restavek program, and which were simply children of the locals.

We made friends with everyone by giving out candy and showing them our drone. They were intrigued by the high-tech gadget, and our helicopter was probably the most incredible thing that happened to them all year. Unlike the reports from the Navy SEALs and other team members who had tried to infiltrate the area, the mood was friendly and peaceful.

Our medical personnel team had just arrived from Port-au-Prince and were taking temperatures, getting nasal swabs, and testing the children's DNA. Jim, Sean, and I told the locals we were there to help organize this healthcare clinic.

Among the hundreds of children in the area, one stood out: a thirteen-year-old girl with a baby of her own. Jim believed she was being trafficked, with the child likely fathered by her captor. While talking privately with some of the kids, Jim showed a photo of Galli to many of them. When the thirteen-year-old mother saw the picture, she exclaimed in Creole, "I know him, I know him! He is much older now, but he still looks the same."

As Jim brought the picture closer to the young girl, her face lit up. She exclaimed, "Oh, yes. Oh, yes, we know him."

Jim asked, "Is his name Galli?"

The girl responded, "No, no. We call him Ali. But that is the same boy."

She continued, "He used to live and work here, but they moved him. He was with us, but they took him to another region." She pointed to a mountain area and said, "He was taken up there."

We were exhilarated! This was the first solid confirmation in years that Galli was still alive since the search for him began. The children did not know him as Galli; they called him "Ali," which made sense. He was taken at four years old, so he might not have been able to communicate his name clearly, or his captors could have changed it. It was logical that a young child might struggle with names, and Ali was close enough to Galli. The girl's confident identification and the details she provided confirmed that the little boy we had been searching for was still out there, now known as Ali.

The traffickers and the local villagers could not learn the real reason for setting up the clinics. The search for Galli had to be kept quiet to ensure his safety and the mission's success. Jim carefully gathered information from the young informant about where she lived and how to contact her. He asked casual questions, mixing them into the conversation to avoid making anyone suspicious.

After gathering as much information as possible from the children, we spent more time visiting with the adults to establish credibility and goodwill with the villagers. This helped us feel confident that we could reach the edge of the jungle area without any problems in the future. With our cover intact, we contacted our helicopter pilot and flew back across the border to the Dominican Republic. The aviation authorities were unaware of our illegal escapades, and the mission was successful. We finally obtained the missing boy's first proof of life.

As the helicopter lifted off, I reflected on the day's events. The image of the girl's hopeful eyes stayed with me. Her information had been a breakthrough in our search for Galli. The mission was far from over, but we now had a significant lead. The next phase of our mission would be dangerous, but we were prepared to face whatever challenges lay in our path to bring the child home.

20

EDGE OF THE WILDERNESS

A Test of Courage

The operator, known on the streets as Andrew Westins, was one of only three operatives bold enough to venture into the depths of the jungle with Jim and me. Andrew had spent years sharpening his skills in combat training, self-defense, undercover work, and escape and evasion. He had been security detail in dozens of undercover operations in some of the most dangerous places on the planet. His massive brother Aaron had joined us on risky missions in Port-au-Prince when we took down the largest trafficking ring, but this time, we needed someone who could pass as a doctor without looking like a security operator.

Andrew would be the perfect match. He could hit like a freight train and offered a level of security far superior to any former military personnel we could have brought along. The key was to blend in while carrying the maximum amount of security. Andrew was the answer.

I called Andrew and described the dangerous mission ahead; I let him know that even the former Navy SEALs could not get close to the jungle area. We had built trust with the locals using the clinic, but there were no guarantees we could safely reach the area where the young informant had told us to go. Without hesitation, Andrew asked, "When are we leaving?" Years later, I bought Andrew a T-shirt that read, "That is a Horrible Idea! What time?" which perfectly captured his attitude and that of other operators who joined us on these missions.

Flying into the remote jungle area by helicopter would attract dangerous attention, and with the closed borders, it was the only way to enter from the Dominican side. We had no choice but to risk flying into Port-au-Prince, Haiti. Jim assured us that we would be protected from the moment we exited the plane. His confidence was reassuring, but the reality of my real persona being known by corrupt political officials was concerning.

Acknowledging the risk, Andrew and I landed in Port-au-Prince, fully prepared for our undercover mission as doctors in the jungle. We arrived with carefully chosen outfits to help us blend in as medical professionals and a handful of supplies to convincingly portray ourselves as doctors.

Jim was there as soon as we stepped off the plane; his immediate presence was calming and disturbing. He swiftly led us to a private room where our immigration papers were processed with unusual speed.

From there, he rapidly escorted us to a secure area where a car awaited. As we approached, two muscular, highly trained Haitian operators stood guard, their eyes carefully scanning the surroundings. They opened our doors with practiced precision, their commanding presence providing a silent but firm feeling of safety despite the tension around us.

"Can I drive?" Andrew asked.

Over the years, Andrew has completed various courses on evasive and defensive driving specifically designed for undercover operators, executive protection, and Secret Service agents. He is one of the most skilled high-speed defensive drivers I know, skilled at maneuvering through ambushes and evading surprise attacks. His extensive training lets him intuitively interpret and respond to his vehicle's feedback in risky situations, such as planned assaults and sudden ambushes. Andrew's expertise allows him to remain calm and execute precise actions under pressure, ensuring the safety and success of our missions.

With the recent surge in violence and carjackings in the region, coupled with the reality that I now had political enemies in the country, I voiced my agreement that Andrew should take over as our driver instead of the federal guard. The situation had become increasingly dangerous, and Andrew's specialized training in evasive driving and handling high-risk scenarios made him the ideal choice for our safety. His ability to anticipate and respond to potential threats on the road far surpassed that of the average driver, ensuring we would have the best possible protection during our journey.

Port-au-Prince was unquestionably the most dangerous place for me and Andrew in Haiti, given our three months of undercover work there, along with the government corruption and political instability. Recognizing these risks, we decided to avoid the city altogether. Instead, we arranged to travel with our security team for five hours, heading towards the jungle's edge. From that point, we would proceed on foot. This strategy reduced our exposure to urban threats and enabled us to reach our desired destination more quickly.

The following five hours would be spent navigating winding dirt roads, driving deep into Haiti's mountainous regions. Interestingly, "Haiti" means "land of high mountains," a fitting description given the country's rugged terrain. The peaks in Haiti soar from approximately 6,000 feet to nearly 9,000 feet in elevation. As we ascended from the airport in Port-au-Prince, the landscape dramatically transformed, with towering mountains rising majestically around us.

After hours of driving, we finally found a place to rest for the night. We were now near the jungle and, so far, had not run into any of the troubles the Navy SEALs faced during their earlier mission. Andrew and I put on medical scrubs to blend in and avoid suspicion, ready to pretend to be medical professionals if questioned. We planned to mention the clinic we had set up a few weeks before, saying we were back for follow-up visits. This cover story was meant to reassure the locals and let us move safely through the area without drawing unwanted attention. As we settled in for the night, we stayed alert, knowing there would be challenges ahead in this unpredictable terrain.

The following day, we started early. Once again, we dressed in our blue scrubs and set out toward the end of the road, right at the edge of the wilderness. The excitement built as we finally arrived at the elusive jungle's edge, a milestone none of the undercover operators before us had reached. This was quite literally the end of the road. From here, our journey would become even more challenging. We had to choose: continue on foot or find horses to ride through the dense and treacherous jungle terrain.

Standing at the threshold of the jungle, we took a moment to absorb the importance of our mission. The thick canopy of trees loomed ahead, with the sounds of wildlife creating an almost eerie soundtrack to our thoughts. We knew the path forward would be a journey into the unknown, but we were determined to press on.

Our two top-tier security personnel had come with us from the airport, armed with handguns and assault rifles to handle any potential threats. They were seasoned professionals, always confident and ready during our journey. However, as we reached the edge of the wilderness, I noticed a change in their demeanor. The bold and confident security guards now showed signs of fear and hesitation about going any further.

It was as if the dense, dark jungle ahead had drained their courage. Their eyes, once sharp and focused, now darted nervously, scanning the unfamiliar terrain. The rumors of the danger in the jungle controlled by the drug lords and cartels were more than they could bear.

"This is the end of the road," stated Rocky, one of the security guards. "We do not go any farther." His concern was evident in his eyes.

"The road has ended, but our mission is just beginning," Jim countered. "This is why we are here, to follow up on the leads that can only be done in the wilderness area!"

Realizing the seriousness of the situation, Jim gathered the team for a brief but critical talk. Morale had clearly dropped, and we needed to boost their resolve. "We've come this far," Jim said firmly, making eye contact with each person. "We knew this would not be easy, but we are prepared. We have a mission to complete, and we must rely on our training and each other to get through this."

Jim reminded them of all the work it took to get here. The medical clinic was carefully designed to earn the trust of the locals, hoping that the drug lords in the jungle would hear about us as doctors. We had spent the last few days flying and driving, coming to the jungle to follow up on the leads and find the missing child.

Jim spoke Creole, Haiti's native language, and was the main contact with the girl from the clinic who recognized Galli. It was crucial for him to be in the jungle. Andrew and I, posing as American doctors, were there to provide cover for him. After some thought, we realized that not having a security team with us might be less threatening to the cartel.

I approached the security team and asked, "Would you be okay if Andrew, Jim, and I continued without you?"

"Absolutely not!" countered Rocky. "I am responsible for your safety. That jungle is more dangerous than your undercover work in the city."

Despite our best efforts to rally the team, we could see the concern in our security personnel. Their faces, once confident, now showed dread. They were not just afraid for their own lives; they were insistent that Andrew, Jim, and I should not go further into the jungle either.

This was not just a mission anymore but a test of our courage and commitment. The path ahead was dangerous, and we needed to dig deep into our strength. Looking around at our team, we knew we had to find a way around their fear. We had come too far to stop here.

I pulled Andrew aside and whispered, "What do we do? They won't let us go any further, with or without them. They are obviously terrified of whatever lies beyond the edge of this jungle, but we need a way to convince them to let us go without them."

"It is their pride," observed Andrew. "They do not want to look like cowards if they stay behind while we go on."

Jim's fluency in Creole and his connection with the girl were crucial. Andrew and I knew the risks but also saw the need to move forward without the added threat of armed guards. The cartel would be less likely to see us as a threat if we looked vulnerable.

Then I had an idea. We returned to the security team and said, "You guys are right; this area is very dangerous. If we all enter the jungle, no one will be here to watch our car and luggage. No doubt it will all be stolen by the time we get back. Would you mind staying behind to protect the vehicle and everything? You can keep a radio here, and we will contact you if anything goes wrong. Also, there is a bit of a cell signal here, so Andrew and I will share our locations with you. If we separate without notifying you, you will know something is wrong."

Rocky looked uneasy, his concern evident. "We can't be responsible if something goes wrong," he pleaded.

I took a deep breath and tried to convey the seriousness of our mission. "Rocky, we need to blend in. Armed guards will only draw attention. Trust us; we know how to handle ourselves."

Rocky's jaw clenched, his eyes filled with worry and frustration. He knew the dangers but also understood our resolve. Finally, with a heavy sigh, he nodded.

The other operator followed Rocky's acceptance. This plan gave them an essential role without facing immediate danger, allowing us to move forward. As we prepared to enter the jungle, I felt a mix of relief and anticipation. The true test of our resolve was just beginning.

21

DOCTORS IN THE JUNGLE

Unarmed in Dangerous Territory

"Take my gun," Rocky pleaded, his voice filled with desperation as we saddled up the horses under the dim light of dawn. It will help ensure your safety."

I shook my head, tightening the straps on my saddle. "I think we will be safer without it. Doctors do not carry guns on charity missions."

Rocky looked at me with a mix of fear and frustration. He knew the dangers ahead, dangers we chose to face unarmed. The tension was real as Jim, Andrew, and I finished getting the horses ready. The morning mist hung over the hillside, hiding the path that led into the dense jungle below.

We mounted our horses, the leather creaking under our weight, and started the careful descent. The trail was steep and covered with loose rocks, making every step risky. But the horses moved gracefully, their sure footing giving us some comfort in the growing anxiety.

The canopy thickened as we went further down, and the air became heavier with the smell of damp earth and decaying leaves. The reality of our situation settled in; we were entering uncharted territory where the cartel wrote the rules.

Each step deeper into the valley felt like a step away from safety and toward an uncertain fate. The trail narrowed, surrounded by thick bushes and tall trees. We were vulnerable and exposed, and the feeling of being watched grew stronger with each passing moment.

I glanced back at Jim. His face showed determination, but there was unease in his eyes. The unspoken question was on our minds: Would we be met with hostility or a warm welcome? The answer lay somewhere in the depths of the jungle, in the heart of the cartel-controlled area we now dared to enter.

Hours later, we finally arrived at the area described by the young girl who claimed to know Galli. Jim approached the village men and explained that we were there as an extension of the medical clinic we hosted a few weeks ago. Our mission was to ensure that all the children in the area were healthy. Andrew and I set up under a grass-roof hut while Jim encouraged the men to bring the children in from the fields.

We unpacked thermometers and a stethoscope to make our setup look as professional as possible. The children began lining up, each one waiting patiently to be examined. We were especially hoping to see the thirteen-year-old mother who had said she knew the missing boy from the church house.

The children came to our makeshift table in the jungle one by one. We took their temperatures and listened to their breathing through the stethoscope. As a parting gesture, Andrew handed out cough drops from his bag of goodies. It was not the most sophisticated doctor setup, but it was all we could carry into the jungle. Our main priority was getting more intel on the missing boy, Galli.

Finally, we saw her—the thirteen-year-old girl with a baby on her hip. The baby's father was likely one of the children's captors. Jim gently pulled her aside to learn more about Galli and where he might have been taken. We had to be extremely cautious not to arouse any suspicion among the adults in the village.

The girl's eyes darted nervously as Jim spoke with her in hushed tones. Andrew and I continued our examinations, pretending everything was normal. The jungle seemed to close in around us, the weight of our true mission pressing heavily on our minds. The villagers watched us closely, their expressions unreadable.

As Jim talked to the girl, we watched the villagers, scanning for any signs of distrust or hostility. Every glance, every whisper felt like a potential threat. The margin for error was slim; we knew we had to get the information we needed without drawing too much attention.

Jim finally rejoined us, an excited look on his face. He had learned something, but there was no time to discuss it here. We had to finish our work and leave the village without raising any alarms. Our cover as doctors was thin, and any mistake could jeopardize our mission and our lives.

We wrapped up our examinations and packed our equipment, thanking the villagers for their cooperation. As we mounted our horses and began the journey back through the jungle, we could not shake the feeling that we were being watched. The path ahead was uncertain, but we were one step closer to finding Galli. And we knew that every step counted.

As we quietly rode our horses back through the seemingly endless jungle trails, the tranquility was suddenly shattered by the sound of a motorcycle approaching. We looked up and recognized the young man on the bike; he was the same kid who had helped us in the Dominican Republic a few weeks earlier when we were trying to cross the border. He had advised us that our car would not make it and had shown us where to rent motorcycles to get through.

As he pulled up beside us, he expressed his delight that many children had come to our clinic after he spread the news. His energy was positive and helpful. We could tell he was not one of the drug lords; he was probably working for them and transporting things across the border, but he was a good kid.

Jim decided to ask for his help in finding the missing boy. Without revealing that the boy was kidnapped, Jim simply showed him the picture to see if he recognized him. Remembering his previous helpfulness and seeing no threat, Jim trusted him to help us again.

To our surprise, he did! The young man confirmed what the girl had said about the boy being named Ali and having lived there before and knew where Ali might be living now. He offered to take us there or even go in himself to get a picture so we could verify if it was really him.

He said it would take a few days to get there, and the timing was not good at the moment, but he was confident he knew exactly where the boy was taken.

Jim was leading the investigation and exchanged information with the young man. He was determined that we would return and be guided to where Galli was likely living. With renewed hope, we pressed on, knowing we were one step closer to finding the missing boy.

As we continued the trek on horseback, the dense jungle gradually gave way to more familiar terrain. The hours seemed to stretch endlessly, each moment filled with anticipation of what lay ahead. Finally, we reached the jungle's edge and saw our vehicles in the distance.

Our security team, anxiously awaiting our return, greeted us with excitement and surprise. They were amazed that we had navigated the treacherous jungle trails without any incidents. Relief washed over us as we dismounted our horses and began sharing the details of our journey.

The team's energy was encouraging, and we felt a genuine sense of progress for the first time in a while. Jim shared the young man's promise to guide us to Galli's location, and the team quickly began planning our next steps. The jungle had tested our resolve, but we had emerged stronger and more determined than ever.

As the sun began to set, casting long shadows over the landscape, we gathered around to discuss our strategy. The path ahead was still dangerous, but we were united in our mission. The pieces were finally coming together, and we knew that with the right approach, we had a real chance of bringing Galli home.

Jim was a man on a mission; he was the primary contact for both the thirteen-year-old mother and the young man on the motorcycle. He kept in touch with them, coordinating with Andrew and me about the best time to return for our extended jungle trip.

Jim was also deeply involved in exposing the corruption within the Haitian political system. With the large trafficking rings in the country dismantled and the corrupt federal judges disbarred, he was uncovering just how deep the corruption went. Civil unrest was at an all-time high, and those like Jim, fighting corruption, faced constant danger.

Several people in Jim's line of work had met mysterious ends, often dying from sudden heart attacks that many suspected were not natural. Despite the obvious signs of foul play, little was done to investigate these deaths, leaving a cloud of fear and uncertainty over those continuing the fight against corruption. Jim knew the risks, but his dedication to justice and the well-being of the innocent kept him pushing forward, determined to see his mission through to the end.

22

THE ULTIMATE SACRIFICE

A Fallen Hero – Promises to Keep

A few months before, Jim had looked me in the eye and said with unwavering determination, "I do not care if I lose my job, I do not care if I lose my life, I am going to clean up the corruption in my country." His words resonated deeply, reflecting his unyielding commitment to justice despite the enormous risks.

After returning from a jungle operation, Andrew and I had to fly to Mexico to meet with the former Mexican President about ongoing child rescue missions. While we were in Mexico, my phone rang. It was my good friend, retired Navy SEAL Dave Lopez, head of the security teams in Haiti.

"Paul, I have some terrible news," Dave said. A wave of anxiety gripped me, my heart sinking as I imagined the worst.

"Are you sitting down?" Dave continued.

"Yes," I responded, quickly finding a place to sit. "What's going on?"

"Jim is dead. A mysterious heart attack took him."

Shock washed over me, followed swiftly by a torrent of grief and anger. It felt surreal, like a cruel twist of fate. Jim, who had fought so bravely against the corruption that plagued his country, was now gone. The heart attack was suspicious, mirroring the pattern of deaths that had claimed the lives of others fighting the same battle. Deep down, we knew it was not a natural death.

As the reality of Jim's death settled in, a heavy weight pressed on my chest. The loss was not just personal; it was a blow to the cause we had fought for together. Memories of Jim's fierce dedication and unwavering spirit flooded my mind. He had been more than a colleague; he was a friend, a mentor, and a bright beam of hope in a dark world.

But amid the sorrow and anger, a firm resolve began to form. Jim had known the risks and faced them head-on. His death could not be in vain. We had to continue his mission, not just for him but for every innocent life at stake. The fight against corruption and injustice was far from over, and now, it was more personal than ever.

I shared the shocking news with Andrew and the rest of our team, each dealing with the loss in our own way. The atmosphere was heavy with grief but also charged with a renewed determination. Jim's legacy would drive us forward, fueling our resolve to see his mission through. The path ahead was dangerous, but we owed it to Jim and the children to keep fighting, no matter the cost.

Jim was the only person in Port-au-Prince that I truly trusted. Returning unaccompanied would be extremely dangerous. However, there was one final trip to the city that I had to make. Regardless of the risk, I needed to be at Jim's funeral. We needed his family to know we supported him and loved him. This would be extremely risky, but we had to return for Jim's sake.

Returning to Haiti for Jim's funeral was more challenging than any mission I had ever undertaken. The emotional toll was immense, but my commitment to fighting for good and honoring our fallen team members kept me going. Dave Lopez flew with me, partly to ensure my safety and partly to support each other through this difficult time.

As we arrived in Haiti, the reality of Jim's absence hit me even harder. The familiar sights and sounds of the country stood out sharply against the emptiness left by his death. At the funeral, Dave and I stood with his family, sharing their sorrow and showing our support. The ceremony was beautiful, filled with tears and heartfelt speeches about a man who had given everything for his cause. Because of his dedicated service, hundreds of children were now back with their families.

In that moment, surrounded by the people Jim had loved and protected, we felt a renewed sense of purpose. The fight against corruption and injustice was far from over, and now, it was even more personal. Jim's spirit would guide us, and his memory would inspire us to push forward, no matter the risks.

I knew that our mission had taken on a new meaning. We were no longer just fighting for the innocent; we were fighting for Jim and the values he stood for. The road ahead was challenging, but our resolve was stronger than ever. We would continue the fight for Jim, his family, and all those who believed in a better future. Unfortunately, because of ever-shifting conditions in Haiti for the worse, we were never able to return to find Galli and rescue him. He is still among the missing, his fate unknown.

After the funeral, we made our way back to the airport, our hearts heavy with the weight of loss and the memories of Jim. As we stood in line for security, I noticed something unusual that seemed almost out of place amid my sorrow. A stunning Colombian girl stood in the security line behind me. Her radiant presence cut through the gloom, drawing my attention.

Striking up a conversation, I discovered she was on a medical charity mission to help children in Haitian orphanages. To my amazement, she had supported one of the foundations Dave and I were working with. She was a well-known Colombian actress named Hada Vanessa who had dedicated the last few weeks to aiding the children of Haiti. Her passion for the cause was evident in every word she spoke, and I found myself captivated by her dedication and warmth.

We spoke for the next hour, waiting for our plane. Our conversation flowed effortlessly, covering topics close to our hearts: charity work, rescue missions, saving children, and healing the world. By what felt like divine chance, her seat on the plane was right behind mine. I tipped my chair back, and we continued our deep conversation for the entire flight back to the US.

The connection we formed was unlike anything I had ever experienced. Her passion for making a difference in the lives of others, especially children, was awe-inspiring. Meeting her was a bright light in the darkness surrounding Jim's death. Her compassion and dedication to helping children resonated with everything I was striving for.

Once we landed in the US, we continued discussing our charity work. Our conversation was so engaging that we both missed our connecting flights. We were too captivated by our discussions to notice the time slipping away. The hours we spent talking were filled with a common purpose and a shared mission that helped ease the pain of losing Jim.

What began as a chance encounter turned into something extraordinary. Hours turned into days and days into weeks. Vanessa and I spent nearly every waking minute together or on the phone, united by our shared goal of helping humanity heal. After meeting in Haiti, we worked side by side, driven by our shared dedication to helping children. Her compassion was not a recent development but a lifelong commitment that began in her youth, perfectly aligning with my passion for the cause.

Vanessa's unwavering devotion and love for the children were genuinely inspiring. Her volunteering stories and her relentless pursuit of justice for the innocent fueled my passion. We began traveling the world together on a full-time philanthropic mission. We spoke to groups of donors, held fundraisers, assisted with safe houses, and even participated in rescue missions together. Each experience strengthened our bond and deepened our shared resolve.

A few months after meeting Vanessa, I was nominated to receive the Ellis Island Medal of Honor for my charity work. It was a formal event, and I planned to wear a tuxedo. Wanting to coordinate, I asked Vanessa what color dress she would wear so I could choose a matching tuxedo from my extensive collection. Then, she told me she did not own a formal gala dress. This was an intriguing contrast to my overflowing two-story closet filled with suits, tuxedos, and shoes I had accumulated over the years.

Determined to find her the perfect dress, I took her to a boutique that sold formal wear for women. She was concerned about spending too much money, but I picked out a beautiful gala dress priced at about $2,000. As we approached the checkout, Vanessa glanced at the price tag, and her eyes widened.

"Paul, what is the average cost of rescuing a trafficked child?" she asked softly.

"It is about $2,000," I replied.

She looked at me with a mix of resolve and compassion. "I am not wearing a child," she exclaimed. "If that money can be used to free a child from slavery, I can't wear that dress. I would much rather get a $200 dress and donate the rest to the Child Liberation Foundation."

At that moment, I was deeply moved by Vanessa's selflessness and unwavering commitment to our cause. Her words and actions reflected a deep empathy and a willingness to put the needs of others above her desires. It was a powerful reminder of the impact one can make by choosing compassion and generosity, and it solidified my admiration and love for her. We left the store with a modest dress and a renewed sense of purpose, knowing our small sacrifice could change a child's life forever.

A few years later, we were married. Her strength and conviction create a solid foundation upon which we have built our family. The darkness of losing Jim had unexpectedly led me to the love of my life. She is now the executive director of the Child Liberation Foundation, working tirelessly every day to heal the world's children. Our lives, brought together by Divine intervention and a shared commitment to justice and compassion, exemplify the enduring power of hope and love.

Jim's legacy lived on through our work and our love. The pain of his loss had given birth to a new chapter, one filled with renewed purpose and the promise of a brighter future. Together, we continued the fight against corruption and injustice, driven by the memory of a friend who had given everything for the cause he believed in. The journey was far from over, but we honored Jim's spirit with each step and carried forward his mission, turning sorrow into a force for good.

Dave, JR, Andrew, Jimmy, Glenn, Joseph, Jeremy, and I, along with many other brave operators, continued our relentless fight against child trafficking. Many of them went on to create their own foundations, branching out from our beginnings with ACTO. Their dedication to this cause was unwavering, each driven by a shared mission to rescue and protect the innocent.

In the future books of The Child Liberation Series, we will continue to shed light on these remarkable warriors and their tireless efforts to combat this great evil. Their stories are not just tales of bravery but a witness to the power of the human spirit and the unyielding fight for justice. Together, we will continue to illuminate the darkness and inspire others to join the battle, ensuring that the legacy of these extraordinary men lives on.

Part IV

Liberating Humanity from Slavery

Creating a Global Impact and Healing the Children

23

IGNITING A GLOBAL MOVEMENT

Transforming Lives Through Film

"So, you are the little woman who wrote the book that made this great war!" President Lincoln remarked upon meeting Harriet Beecher Stowe, the author of *Uncle Tom's Cabin*. In the early 1800s, Stowe's literary work served as a catalyst, shaking the conscience of a nation and leading to the abolition of slavery. Fast-forward more than 150 years to the child rescue operations in this book, and we found ourselves motivated to follow in the footsteps of those who had used the media to expose injustice.

Our missions revealed the grim reality of modern slavery, a shocking revelation that demanded the attention of a world blissfully ignorant of the evil occurring beyond their comfortable lives. The realization that innocent children were being sold into despicable acts ignited a powerful desire within me to shatter the indifference surrounding the issue. I could not turn a blind eye to the horrors we had witnessed.

We needed massive awareness and wanted to create a global movement to combat this modern-day plague. Reflecting on history, it became evident that stories like Stowe's *Uncle Tom's Cabin* had been instrumental in shaping public opinion and driving social change. The power of media, both then and now, was undeniable.

Numerous documentaries were created capturing the rescue missions, but we all understood the importance of reaching a broader audience. To truly demonstrate the reality of the situation, we needed more than just short films. A full-length feature film emerged as the ideal solution, and I pledged to become the primary investor in a movie based on some of the rescue missions our team and I had participated in.

We had no idea this effort would become a complicated journey, facing off against Big Media and Hollywood. Starting this massive project meant dealing with the film industry's monopoly. We had meetings with major studios like Sony, Lionsgate, and Paramount, but some wanted more control over the story than we were willing to give. Not discouraged, I met with some investors and industry leaders, sharing the Colombia rescue and missions in Acapulco, Mexico City, the Dominican Republic, Haiti, and more. Each story was a powerful call for change.

Because of the subject's sensitivity, addressing child trafficking in a film requires a careful and empathetic approach. We needed to find a team that not only possessed filmmaking expertise but also shared a deep understanding of the principles of faith and moral strength that were the foundation of our mission. Creating the story to capture our experiences' emotional journey demanded a special kind of team.

Diligently searching for ways to raise awareness of child trafficking, I began sharing the story with groups of leaders and influencers. Many people who unknowingly played pivotal roles in the journey deserve credit for the movie's eventual global movement. One such person, Brent, opened doors that eventually led me to the film's producers.

I was speaking at a networking group about the profound impact of hearing the "sound of freedom" emanating from the grass hut where the children were held after their rescue in Colombia. During my talk, I recounted my experiences and expressed my deep passion for combating child trafficking. The audience was profoundly moved by what they heard. As a result of this network connection, I was referred to a group organizing a post-Grammy concert event aimed at fighting child trafficking.

The event, "Rock Against Child Trafficking," was attended by renowned figures like Pierce Brosnan and President Vicente Fox and raised money and awareness to combat this plague. Inspired by our rescue stories, the group mobilized support and introduced me to influential people who could assist with our mission.

During the post-Grammy event, I met Eduardo Verastegui, a Mexican actor known for his roles in faith-based films. When he heard of the child rescue missions, his passionate response was, "Hermano, we need to make this into a movie."

In this unexpected journey, Eduardo invited me to watch a film he had recently been a part of, *Little Boy*. Directed by Alejandro Monteverde, the movie explores the themes of faith, perseverance, and the powerful impact a child's innocence can have on those around them. The title symbolizes the child's small stature and unwavering faith in his ability to make a difference.

What happened next was another fantastic coincidence. Alejandro Monteverde was already involved in scripting a fictitious story centered around child trafficking. When he learned about our real-life experiences and the child rescue mission in Colombia, he was deeply moved and expressed a strong interest in contributing to creating a feature film. This partnership resulted in the birth of *Sound of Freedom*. This powerful film intertwines the real-life stories of child trafficking rescue missions with the artistry of Alejandro Monteverde's storytelling. The merging of our mission and Monteverde's creative vision has allowed us to bring attention to the disturbing issue of child trafficking through the emotionally transformational tool of a feature film.

My family's cabin, in the heart of the Rocky Mountains, provided the ideal setting for the scriptwriting journey. Inspired by the collective experiences of numerous operators engaged in global missions, they skillfully intertwined multiple rescue stories to craft a captivating story. While the film prominently features a small group of people, it is essential to recognize that the true honor belongs to countless unsung heroes who persistently toil in the shadows, dedicated to the ongoing mission of rescuing trafficked children.

Midway through completing the script for *Sound of Freedom*, Alejandro's world was shattered by a horrific event. As he passionately penned the details of the rescue missions, tragedy struck his family. His father and brother were brutally kidnapped and held for ransom, eventually murdered by violent criminals. The devastation was immense for Alejandro, his family, and everyone who knew him.

This profound loss nearly halted the script's completion. Yet, Alejandro channeled his grief into a fierce determination to combat evil at its core. He returned to the team with renewed determination and an unwavering commitment to create something transformative, aiming to dismantle the wicked networks preying upon the innocent. Alejandro finished the script, crafting the awe-inspiring masterpiece we cherish today. His tragic loss motivated him to take action to bring this powerful movie to the world.

By March 2017, the script was complete, and we began the search for key actors. With initial rejections from actors like Mark Wahlberg and Hugh Jackman, the introduction to Jim Caviezel, known for his compelling portrayals, emerged as the perfect match for the lead role.

Recognized for portraying Jesus in *The Passion of the Christ*, directed by Mel Gibson, Caviezel's intense and committed performance resonated deeply with a devoted following, particularly among conservative moviegoers. This committed audience later emerged as a driving force in promoting the message behind *Sound of Freedom*.

In the search for the ideal actor to portray my role in the Colombia mission, we considered several notable names, including Ryan Reynolds and Ryan Gosling. The producer of our movie also expressed interest in playing a pivotal role as an actor in addition to his producing duties. After thoughtful discussion, we decided he would portray Pablo Delgado, a character based on me. Pablo is a fund manager who retires from the investment world to dedicate himself to undercover child rescue missions and philanthropy.

Centering on the mission in Cartagena, Colombia, it became evident that filming *Sound of Freedom* close to the location of the actual rescue would add an additional level of authenticity to the film. Even with my initial encounter with Colombia, marked by fear for my safety, my following experiences formed a deep respect and love for the country and its people. Returning to Colombia for the film's production, I discovered a feeling of peace. Our native film crews were committed to spreading our message of hope and liberation to the world.

The process of bringing *Sound of Freedom* to its final, distributable form extended over several years following the completion of filming. Reflecting on the outcome, I felt emotionally divided. The storyline appears to lean heavily on Jim Caviezel's character rather than highlighting the beautiful stories of the rescued children. Even with this observation, the overall execution of the film remained admirable, creating a powerful tool that would create the movement we had envisioned.

Securing distribution for *Sound of Freedom* became challenging as traditional Hollywood channels declined the film because it did not fit their desired narrative. Undiscouraged by the rejections, our primary goal went beyond financial gain; instead, it was rooted in the desire to make a meaningful impact and awaken collective consciousness.

Despite facing challenges, we stayed committed to the project because we believed the film could highlight important issues and inspire positive change. After almost five years of unwavering dedication, a critical turning point occurred when Angel Studios, known for supporting impactful projects like *The Chosen*, joined as the distributor. Their grassroots approach and shared values marked a breakthrough, allowing Sound of Freedom to reach audiences and initiate meaningful conversations. This partnership brought the film to the world and strengthened our belief in media as a powerful force for social change.

Our success in distribution was built on the power of social media and the support of millions of passionate people fighting against evil. This wave of support became so strong that it overpowered the efforts of big media and Hollywood to silence the film. Against all odds, this determination pushed our movie to incredible success, making it the most successful independent film of 2024. It even beat out big box office hits like Indiana Jones and Mission Impossible, symbolizing hope and dedication for everyone who believed in its cause.

I like to say, "*Sound of Freedom* was brought to the people by the people." It became a demonstration of the power of perseverance, faith, and unwavering commitment to exposing and eradicating the darkness that affects the lives of trafficked children worldwide. Our goal was not just a successful movie but the birth of a global movement against the great evil that is child trafficking.

24

KEEPING CHILDREN SAFE AT HOME

Discovering the Epidemic of Childhood Trauma

After watching the *Sound of Freedom* movie, an interviewer asked me, "What can we do to keep our kids safe?"

"Go home and hug your children," I responded.

He followed up with, "That seems too simple; shouldn't we do things like put tracking devices on them or shut down their social media? How does hugging your children prevent trafficking?"

I explained that while many of us think of child trafficking in deeply impoverished countries, we do not realize the dangers in our neighborhoods. The majority of children who are subjected to trafficking in the US come from broken homes, runaways, or a broken foster care program.

"Should trafficking and kidnapping be the biggest concern for parents wanting to keep their children safe?" The interviewer asked.

"No," I answered. "The biggest threat to children isn't being taken from their homes; it's the dangers they face within them. Child abuse is a global epidemic, affecting everyone either directly or indirectly. About one in four women were sexually abused as children, and one in seven children experiences some abuse or neglect each year. This means that if you step outside and look at the homes on your street, it's likely that one of them is a dangerous place for children. As a parent, your top priority should be to create a physically and emotionally safe space for your children to grow up."

I continued, "Your children need to feel comfortable coming to you and saying, 'Mom, I do not like it when you tell me to hug Uncle Harry because he rubs me weird and says we should keep secrets from you.' or 'Dad, I do not want to go to this friend's house because her big brother takes pictures of us changing and he says sexual things to me' or 'The new babysitter is showing us pornography and telling us we should trust her more than you.' These are grooming behaviors, and our children's intuition is more accurate than we give them credit for."

In high school, I was chosen to serve as the president of the Peer Leadership Team (PLT). This role tasked me with creating a safe space within the school and supporting students struggling with addictions, depression, and home life issues. I assembled a dedicated team, and we underwent extensive training as peer counselors. We acquired skills to assist students dealing with drug and alcohol addictions, suicidal thoughts, and domestic abuse. Our mission was to build a supportive environment for troubled youth and be there for those in need.

While I was serving in this role, I began to see the level of trauma many children go through in their own homes. So many of these troubled teens were abused as children, and they had nowhere to turn. If the student shared these stories with a teacher, the law required the educator to take it to the authorities. This meant many teens were afraid to reveal any issues they had at home. We, as peer counselors, were able to bridge this gap by giving the kids someone they were not afraid to talk to, and we could encourage them to get the necessary help from authorities when appropriate. If they did not have a compassionate peer counselor, most of them held the pain inside without ever talking about it.

Partway through my senior year of high school, the vice principal entered my first-period advanced placement Calculus class. We had just been handed a test representing a large percentage of our grade.

After speaking privately with her, my teacher walked straight to my desk, wrote an "A" on the top of my test, and said, "Paul, your skills are needed to help some of the other students."

As we walked down the hallway, the Vice Principal said, "I have some very sad news. One of the popular sophomore kids committed suicide last night, and the other students are just learning about it." She said, "We need to help them deal with the emotional trauma. You and your team have been trained to handle tragedies like this, and we need you, along with the adult crisis counselors, to provide emotional support."

It was heartbreaking to learn of the problems this student had at home before taking his own life. I found myself wishing we had been able to provide the emotional support for him to heal before it got to this point. Now, the only thing we could do was to comfort grieving students through an extremely difficult time.

Serving as a peer counselor, it became evident that over two-thirds of all children had experienced a traumatic event by the time they were sixteen years old. Most of them try to bury their pain, and it comes out in the form of anxiety, shame, depression, anger, and low self-esteem. Unfortunately, some trauma leads to substance abuse and unhealthy sexual behaviors. Others allow poor choices, combined with their unresolved trauma, to pass on their pain to others in the form of emotional, verbal, or physical abuse and, in some cases, the abuse of a child.

Giving teenagers the tools to heal helps to prevent a lifetime of pain. The average age of someone speaking out about their abuse as a child is *fifty-two years old*. Most people either have a subconscious block that causes them not to remember the abuse, or they choose to silently hold their pain inside for many years, never releasing it, thereby allowing it to affect every part of their lives. Simply speaking about the trauma offers powerful healing. It is essential to release the pain and recognize that you are not defined by what happened to you or even the things you did. Everything can be healed, and we can all transform our lives into a place of freedom, peace, and personal growth.

If you ever suspect someone you know is suffering from abuse, it is essential to approach a conversation with them delicately and with compassion. Choose a private and comfortable setting to speak with them and focus on creating an atmosphere of trust. Start the conversation with empathy, expressing genuine concern for their well-being. You might say, "I have noticed you seem to be going through a tough time, and I want you to know I am here for you without judgment."

As the conversation unfolds, employ active listening and open-ended questions to allow the person to share their feelings at their own pace. Avoid making assumptions or accusations, and always maintain a non-confrontational tone. For instance, you could express observations without placing blame, saying, "I have noticed some changes in your behavior, and I am concerned about your well-being. Can you share what has been going on?"

Listen attentively without judgment, allowing them to disclose as much or as little as they feel comfortable sharing. Refrain from pressuring them to reveal details they are not ready to discuss. Assure them your goal is to support and help, not force them into anything they are unprepared for.

If they do disclose abuse, believe in and validate their experiences. Tell them it is not their fault and emphasize your commitment to supporting them. Provide information about resources such as helplines, counseling services, or support groups. Encourage them to seek professional help, highlighting its positive impact on their healing process.

Throughout the conversation, maintain discretion, assuring them you will keep the information private unless there is an immediate risk to their safety. Respect their choices and privacy, reinforcing the idea they are in control of their decisions.

Approaching the conversation with sensitivity and empathy establishes a foundation of trust, increasing the likelihood the person will feel comfortable seeking the support they need. Remember, your role is one of support and understanding, and your compassionate approach can make a significant difference in their journey toward healing. Regularly check in with them, reinforcing your ongoing support and willingness to help in any way you can.

If a child (or youth) ever discloses abuse to you, you might feel shocked and at a loss for words, but you must let them know that you are glad that they told you, that they did the right thing, that you believe them, and that they are not to blame in any way for the abuse. After this conversation, you should immediately take steps to ensure the child's safety.

Research shows that how you react to someone who is revealing abuse can have a direct impact on their recovery, which is why responding correctly is so essential. Remember to stay calm and create a safe space for the child to talk to you. Tell them they are doing the right thing by talking to you. At first, it might be difficult to believe a child who has disclosed abuse, especially if you know the abuser. However, you should always ensure the child feels like you believe them. Talking about abuse is very difficult, and it is extremely rare for children to lie about this.

As the child talks to you, do not push them for details or to describe certain events. Just listen and make sure they feel safe, cared for, and understood. Thank them for their bravery in telling you, and ensure they understand that no abuse they suffer is their fault. (Often, children are told by the abuser that what they are experiencing is their fault or that they are to blame for it.) Do not promise that things will immediately improve; instead, let them know you will help and support them.

Regardless of how much you might want to, it is a bad idea to confront the abuser yourself, and you should leave this to the authorities. Additionally, confronting the abuser before law enforcement has a handle on the situation could put the child in more danger.

Overall, suppose you ever find yourself in this situation. In that case, you have the responsibility to care for this child, and you can make one of the most powerful impacts on their life by handling this well and ensuring that they are cared for, trusted, and helped.

Early intervention is key in addressing the effects of trauma. Identifying and addressing the signs of distress early can prevent the development of more serious mental health issues later on and can prevent the abuse from reoccurring. Recognizing signs of emotional distress in children who have experienced sexual abuse is crucial for their protection and recovery. While individual responses can vary, common signs may include the following:

Behavioral Signs

1. **Regression:** Going back to younger behaviors like bed-wetting or thumb-sucking.
2. **Sleep problems:** Nightmares, trouble sleeping, or fear of going to bed.
3. **Eating changes:** Losing appetite or overeating.
4. **Avoidance:** Staying away from certain people or places, especially those linked to the abuser.
5. **Sexual behaviors:** Knowing too much about sex or acting out sexual behaviors.
6. **Aggression or withdrawal:** Unexplained anger or aggression or becoming very quiet and isolated.

Emotional Signs

1. **Anxiety:** Feeling more scared, worried, or nervous.
2. **Depression:** Persistent sadness, losing interest in things they used to enjoy, or feeling hopeless.
3. **Guilt or shame:** Feeling guilty or ashamed about the abuse.
4. **Low self-esteem:** Negative self-talk or feeling worthless.
5. **Mood swings:** Rapid changes in mood without a clear reason.

Physical Signs

1. **Unexplained injuries:** Bruises, bleeding, or soreness around private areas.

2. **Chronic pain:** Complaints of stomachaches, headaches, or other pains without a clear cause.

3. **Frequent infections:** Repeated urinary tract infections or sexually transmitted infections.

Social Signs

1. **School problems:** Dropping in grades or not wanting to attend school.

2. **Relationship issues:** Problems making or keeping friends or suddenly changing friends.

3. **Trust issues:** Difficulty trusting others, including adults and authority figures.

Psychological Signs

1. **Dissociation:** Zoning out or seeming disconnected from their surroundings.

2. **Flashbacks:** Reliving the trauma or having intrusive memories.

3. **Self-harm:** Engaging in self-injurious behavior like cutting or burning.

If you suspect a child is experiencing emotional distress due to sexual abuse, it is essential to take their disclosures seriously and seek help from professionals trained in child trauma and abuse.

The key to healing humanity starts in our homes, where trust, safety, and emotional well-being are established. Children represent the future of our society, and their safety, both physical and emotional, should be our top priority. By paying attention to our children's lives and addressing the root causes of child trauma, we can build a generation of healthy adults and stop the cycle of abuse that is so widespread in our communities. We must take collective action to protect and support our children, ensuring they grow up in safe and loving environments.

25

BEYOND THE RESCUE

The Ripple Effect of Our Actions

A s we each do our part to help humanity heal from the horrors of human trafficking and sexual abuse, we must all take a careful inventory of the ways we contribute to the negativity in our world. It is not just harmful physical actions that can bring pain to others; how we conduct business, treat our families, and direct our energy toward others can have equally damaging effects.

There is something I call the "Tension Transfer" principle, which describes how pain, anxiety, and stress can move from one person to another. Imagine your boss at work is under financial strain. He vents his frustration on you. You carry that stress home and, still reeling from your boss's reprimand, you pick a fight with your spouse over something trivial. Your spouse then takes out their frustration on your child, who kicks the dog, perpetuating a cycle of transferred tension.

Now, imagine you are the boss, and you cruelly yell at an employee who is already on the brink of an emotional breakdown. What you don't know is that this employee was abused as a child and is holding onto unresolved trauma. Additionally, his wife recently left him due to his insatiable pornography addiction, and he is drowning his sorrows in alcohol. Though he has never hurt a child, a combination of his childhood trauma and poor decisions has brought him to the edge. Your harsh behavior becomes the final straw, pushing him over. Tragically, in this case, and many others, it leads to the abuse of a child.

We must each take responsibility for our actions and realize their impact on everything in our lives. What we do often creates a chain reaction, affecting far more than our immediate surroundings. We must try to add positivity instead of contributing to pain and suffering. By being careful with our words and actions, we can help create the environment we want to live in, built on kindness, respect, and empathy.

As adults, compassion for ourselves and others is a powerful tool for breaking the cycle of pain. When someone hurts us, our natural reaction might be to lash out in anger or hold onto our negative feelings. This response can cause us to spread that negativity to others, leading to a ripple effect of hurt feelings and broken relationships. Holding onto anger can make us more likely to act out in ways that harm others, even if we do not realize it. Many times, our children are the victims of unhealed adults.

Many people carry deep-seated trauma that manifests in various ways. Some cope by overeating, while others struggle with addictions to drugs, alcohol, or pornography. Unhealed trauma can also express itself through anger, depression, or anxiety. Understanding that most people have inner wounds can help us be more supportive and less judgmental.

My first understanding of this principle came from an experience with a neighbor named Tommy when I was young. Tommy was eight years older than me and had a mental disability, but despite our age difference and his challenges, we were good friends. Through my friendship with Tommy, I learned the invaluable lesson of letting go of judgment. I came to appreciate and see the light within him, regardless of how different he was from others. Tommy's unique perspective and kind heart taught me to embrace people for who they truly are, beyond any shallow differences or what society expects. This early lesson in compassion and acceptance has stayed with me throughout my life, reminding me of the beauty in diversity and the importance of seeing the worth in every person.

One impactful event with Tommy occurred when I was only six years old. Tommy and I were playing in the park near my house when we had a terrible idea. We ran to hide behind the large willow tree as we saw a Blue Volkswagen Bug come around the corner from the church parking lot. As the VW Bug drew even with us, we cupped our hands around our mouths and yelled, "Fat elephant!"

The shout was directed at the kind, overweight lady driving past us in the car. Tommy had suggested shouting when she drove by, and I thought it sounded fun at the time, but was startled at the emotional pain on her face as she passed us.

Tommy remained unaware of the potential distress our actions may have caused the woman, and I was too young to give it due consideration. However, witnessing the pain in her eyes stirred sadness in my heart, teaching me a valuable life lesson. I realized how our words and actions possess the genuine capacity to inflict pain on others. As I have matured, I have embraced a commitment to living in a way that brings joy to those around me.

Abiding by this principle is not always convenient and presents its fair share of challenges. While most of us strive to be good and kind, we must acknowledge that some choices have brought sadness or pain to others. We must learn to forgive ourselves and forgive others as we strive to transcend our weaknesses and evolve into the best version of ourselves. Each day presents an opportunity to learn, grow, and forgive. I am grateful for the chance to renovate my life and to assist others in doing the same.

We find it easy to look down on others, often judging them for their physical appearance, financial status, social standing, or personal beliefs. We criticize people for being overweight, having addictions, or committing sins that differ from our own. We judge those who exhibit socially unacceptable behavior, such as prostitutes, without realizing that many are victims of trafficking. It's also common to judge socially awkward, disruptive, or angry people without considering the underlying issues in their lives that may contribute to these behaviors. Recognizing the complexities of people's circumstances can lead to greater empathy and understanding.

In the journey to understand human behavior, there is one fundamental truth. If we ever judge another human being, whether it is for being overweight, someone cutting you off on the freeway, or even someone working as a prostitute, there is a 100 percent chance we do not have all the facts to make any judgment. Our initial perceptions are often limited, and we do not know the full extent of what someone else might be going through.

For instance, we do not know if the overweight woman with social anxiety was abused as a child. She might have a medical condition that has caused her to gain weight. Or she could be stuck in an unhealthy relationship, turning to food for comfort and escape. There might be deep trauma that affects her, showing up in the problems she faces now. Her struggles today could come from a mix of past experiences, emotional pain, and psychological issues, each one adding to the challenges she deals with.

You don't know if the guy cutting you off on the freeway is rushing to the hospital for a dying family member. His actions, though seemingly reckless, could be driven by an urgent and dire situation. Perhaps he is in a state of panic or desperation, trying to reach someone in need. Or, he might be an inconsiderate person who disregards the safety of others. The point is that we can't make a fair judgment without knowing all the facts. And nobody but God knows everything that has transpired in someone's life.

Even in the case of someone involved in heinous crimes, such as trafficking, we do not know if that person was a victim of rape or severe abuse during their childhood. Such traumatic experiences can greatly impact a person's actions and choices later in life. Recognizing this complexity in human behavior is crucial in humanity's journey toward understanding and finding real solutions to the problem.

As we discuss the root causes of child abuse and trafficking, it's crucial to emphasize that there is never an excuse for harming a child. My team and I have risked our lives repeatedly to ensure these criminals can never hurt innocent people again. I have zero tolerance or sympathy for those who exploit and harm children.

However, if we are ever going to solve the problem of child trafficking, we have to look deeper than just the surface actions of those involved. We must examine the root causes of a parent selling their child or anyone involved in kidnapping a child. What extreme circumstances or desperate situations lead them to make such a life-shattering decision? Understanding these factors is critical to address the issue at its core.

Additionally, we need to understand why a trafficker would choose this occupation to make money. What societal, economic, or personal pressures push someone towards this criminal path? By uncovering these motivations, we can work towards disrupting the cycle that contributes to trafficking.

If we are going to win this war against child trafficking, we must also confront the demand side of the equation. Why is there even a desire for something so despicable? What cultural, psychological, or economic factors contribute to this horrifying market? Addressing these questions is essential to eliminate the demand that fuels the supply.

While holding people accountable for their crimes and protecting innocence at all costs is essential, instead of solely condemning the people involved, we must work towards understanding the complex factors that lead to such heinous acts. Only then can we hope to create comprehensive solutions that address the root causes and eventually eradicate child trafficking.

26

Hurt People Hurt Others

Healed People Can Heal the World

A decade into the fight against child trafficking has given me deep insights into how to tackle this global issue, revealing both the harsh realities and ineffective approaches. It became clear that simply conducting rescue operations was not enough to stop this evil trade. It's not just about rescuing children; it's about raising the global collective consciousness, dismantling the roots of demand, and helping survivors heal.

Over the years, I have seen the darkest side of humanity and witnessed the light of liberation for those who were once victims. Projects like the *Sound of Freedom* movie have raised global awareness about human trafficking and highlighted this severe issue. However, one major problem remains: the demand from disturbed individuals continues to drive the exploitation and abuse of innocent children. Despite our efforts to stop this crime, the root cause, the twisted desire to harm innocence, remains a considerable challenge.

On every rescue mission, my greatest wish was that we could have arrived earlier, saving the children before they were ever abused. The thought of a time machine often crossed my mind, imagining how we could go back and prevent these horrific crimes from ever occurring. I yearned to have the power to intervene sooner, to be there before the harm was done, and to shield these innocent lives from the trauma they endured. The anguish of knowing we could only help after the fact weighed heavily on my heart, driving me to fight even harder to stop these atrocities from happening in the first place.

Arresting perpetrators is undeniably essential, as it serves as a protective barrier for potential victims. By removing these harmful people from society, we can prevent them from causing further harm. However, a deeper look reveals that the roots of this evil are often embedded in past traumas. These traumas are frequently passed on through generations, creating vicious cycles of abuse. Understanding this, we see that simply arresting offenders is not enough. We must also address the underlying issues that perpetuate this cycle. This involves providing support and resources for healing and breaking the chain of trauma that can lead people to become abusers themselves. By tackling the root causes, we can create a more practical approach to eradicating this problem.

Some people let the pain of their childhood shape how they treat others, perpetuating a cycle of generational trauma and abuse. While many who were abused as children work hard to become protectors of others, it's tragic that over 30 percent of those who were abused go on to become abusers themselves. These statistics, though shocking, only reveal part of the story—many victims suffer in silence. Even with those honorable people who never harm a child, their pain often surfaces in the form of low self-esteem, anxiety, depression, and other emotional scars.

As a global community, our mission is to identify the core of the problem, addressing and healing the underlying traumas before they become a plague passed on to future generations. By doing so, we have the potential to protect children from the cycle of abuse, eradicate trafficking, and heal humanity.

When someone harms a child, it can be attributed to many failures and poor choices along the way. This tragic act comes from a series of very bad decisions, often rooted in negative experiences and unresolved issues. The person involved has likely battled addictions or experienced personal trauma, neglect, or abuse, which contributes to their harmful behavior. A history of suffering and detestable choices influences their actions.

Let me reiterate my unwavering stance on this issue: I am not a sympathizer of anyone who hurts a child. My commitment to protecting children is absolute and uncompromising, and my personal sacrifices in this fight emphasize the seriousness of the issue. However, it is vital to recognize that combating this issue requires a deeper understanding of where these perpetrators are coming from.

Studies show a sad reality: the majority of perpetrators were once victims themselves. Over 68 percent of imprisoned male felons report being traumatized as children, highlighting a disturbing cycle where the abused often become abusers. Family units, which should be sanctuaries of love, frequently hide the distressing reality of sexual violence.

I honor those who never allow their trauma to be passed on to others. These good men and women, who have endured terrible pain and hardship, choose a path of healing and protection rather than perpetuating the cycle of suffering. Instead of allowing their experiences to destroy them, they use their past as a powerful motivator to protect children and ensure that others do not have to endure the same kind of pain they once did. Their strength and compassion shine through as they transform their trauma into a force for good, dedicating themselves to breaking the cycle of abuse and creating a safer, more loving environment for the next generation.

We have the freedom to choose how we respond to our experiences, and this freedom is a fundamental aspect of being human. When we face pain and hardship, we have different options for handling it: we can let our circumstances define us and perpetuate suffering by harming others, or we can release the pain, break the cycle of abuse, and pave the way for healing within our families. Choosing to heal and live fully requires courage, determination, and a commitment to growth.

Embracing a life unburdened by your past is a bold and powerful choice that can break the cycle of generational trauma. This choice ensures that your pain does not pass on to your children in the form of anxiety, depression, or any form of verbal or physical harm. Those who are wounded often wound others, while those who have healed can bring healing to others.

Healing is more than self-improvement; it is a commitment to nurturing and protecting our children, ensuring they grow up free from the shadows of trauma that has affected previous generations. Our mission to eradicate child trafficking and heal humanity begins with addressing this cycle of generational trauma.

In the grand goal of healing humanity, changing our perception and healing the pain of our childhood is not just about finding peace for ourselves. It is about creating a more compassionate and understanding world for everyone. By releasing the pain of our past and finding tools to heal, we contribute to a safer world for our children, ensuring that we stop generational trauma before it ever gets passed on.

Healing generational trauma and breaking the cycle of abuse starts with each of us taking personal responsibility for our own lives. To address the root causes of child abuse and human trafficking, we must consider the emotional impact of our childhood experiences and how they shape us as adults. This is our chance to create a legacy of love and protection that will endure.

Together, we can break the cycle of abuse and create a brighter, safer future for children. We disrupt this cycle when we change our perception of what contributed to our pain. Choosing to let go of negativity does not mean that we accept bad behavior from others. Everyone must be accountable for their actions. But we can release the anger, stop the spread of hurt, and start a new cycle of kindness and understanding.

By choosing a path of self-healing and helping others do the same, we can save millions of children. Healing ourselves and assisting others can indeed transform the entire planet. This is our chance to create a lasting legacy of love and protection. Let's choose to heal, protect, and care with all our passion and strength, breaking the cycle of abuse and ensuring a brighter future for the children.

I urge you to lead your own rescue mission, not just for others but for the child within yourself. Seek healing, embrace forgiveness, and release the chains that bind you. No matter how concealed, the light within every person holds the potential for redemption and change. Hurt people do hurt others, but healed people have the power to heal the world.

27

THE PATH TO HEALING HUMANITY

PTSD, Addictions, Anxiety, and Depression

M ost of us will never know the horror of being trafficked as a child, but we each have unique traumas that need healing. Everyone has experienced pain, and we have all done things that may have hurt others. Forgiving ourselves and releasing the pain of the past is the first and necessary step in healing the world.

Aside from those imprisoned for their crimes and those still enslaved through human trafficking, humanity as a whole is trapped in various forms of bondage, such as addiction, negative emotions, unresolved trauma, and even financial and political oppression. Modern slavery manifests in many ways, preventing us from experiencing true freedom. Liberation is not just a one-time act of rescue; it is an ongoing journey of inner transformation to break free from the chains that bind us.

After a decade of combating this issue, I have come to realize that the solution extends beyond rescuing children from the clutches of traffickers. To truly address the problem, we must help every adult become the child's rescuer within themselves. Initiating a personal rescue mission involves healing, seeking programs and support to overcome childhood trauma, freeing oneself from a lifetime of pain, and forgiving the past.

Each of us has a child within who is hurt, carrying pain, and in need of healing. Changing the world begins with an honest look at ourselves. We must make a conscious effort to heal our broken inner child. We all have chains in different parts of life, whether as victims or offenders. We can create substantial changes by examining our lives, committing to healing ourselves, and getting help when needed.

Studies have found that children who experience trauma, whether it be sexual trauma, verbal abuse, or witnessing domestic violence, are about three times more likely to develop mental health issues as adults compared to those who do not experience such suffering. The impact of these early traumatic experiences can be severe, shaping a person's emotional and psychological health throughout their entire life.

Young children who endure abusive experiences are at a much higher risk of developing anxiety, depression, and other mental health disorders. Their developing brains are especially vulnerable to the stresses and strains of traumatic events. Unfortunately, most childhood trauma goes undetected and unreported, affecting every area of life well into adulthood.

Understanding the relationship between childhood trauma and mental health is essential. While it is true that childhood trauma can have lifelong impacts, it is equally important to recognize that experiencing trauma does not always lead to the development of mental health issues. The human spirit is incredibly strong, and many people are able to heal through the pain and never experience the adverse effects of trauma.

In my early twenties, I started a marketing company that specialized in helping people overcome PTSD, anxiety, and depression disorders using a personal coaching program. This aligned with my passion for contributing to the healing and well-being of others. It was a perfect way to use the experience I had gained during high school, where I dedicated most of my free time to supporting fellow students through difficult times.

Our program was based on a cognitive restructuring approach to help people change habits and negative thinking patterns that were contributing to their anxiety and depression. The audio program was featured in an infomercial, where we witnessed the overwhelming response of those seeking help, with more than 50,000 calls per month from those suffering from these conditions. Our company provided ongoing support calls and guided those facing challenges toward additional assistance.

Although our firm had over 200 employees and managing them was a full-time job, I prioritized personally speaking with many of our customers over the phone. There was great satisfaction in helping others overcome their self-limiting beliefs, empowering them to recognize their potential, and breaking free from anxiety and depression. I spoke with thousands of individuals suffering from debilitating anxiety and depression, and each conversation was both heartbreaking and deeply rewarding.

"I have sabotaged every healthy relationship that comes into my life, and I can't remember the last time I looked in the mirror and smiled," cried a sixty-year-old woman on the phone. "My chest feels like I am ready to have a heart attack whenever I am around unfamiliar people, and I wake up every morning feeling hopeless."

Unfortunately, I encountered variations of this story countless times from people wrestling with severe mental health challenges. As they pleaded for liberation from their pain, many revealed the tragic connection between their emotional struggles and sexual abuse as a child. It was sad to witness the same issues I had encountered in high school now afflicting millions of adults—a true *epidemic of unresolved childhood trauma.*

For those who are holding onto deep childhood trauma, it is essential to recognize that there are many resources available to help you heal. Therapy, support groups, facilitated healing retreats, and self-help strategies can all play a valuable role in your journey toward recovery. Taking the time to address and release the pain of the past is essential for your well-being and those around you. By letting go of what does not belong to you, you create space for a more fulfilled and peaceful life. Most importantly, you ensure that the toxic energy of unhealed trauma does not get passed on to others, breaking the cycle of pain and creating a path for a healthier future.

Sadly, even with the severity of mental health struggles, they are often not openly discussed, leading to a common misconception that they are rare. In reality, mental health issues are far more prevalent than many people realize. In any given year, 26 percent of adults in the United States—about one in four—suffer from a diagnosable mental disorder. The stigma surrounding mental health can contribute to feelings of isolation and shame, preventing people from seeking the help they need.

As I built the anti-anxiety and depression marketing company, we realized that the very thing we were fighting stopped many people from getting the help they needed. Their worry, what-if thinking, and negative expectations prevented them from using our tools to heal. We realized a key element was missing: *Belief.* Overcoming all anxiety and depression was challenging without genuine *confidence* in the possibility of healing.

Identifying this, we created an opportunity to connect our clients with a compassionate, understanding mentor who had overcome similar challenges using our program. This combination empowered them with the most valuable tool for personal change—the *belief* that they *could* genuinely heal.

When someone suffers from anxiety and depression stemming from sexual or emotional trauma, it can become debilitating. When paired with a facilitator or a personal coach who has experienced similar challenges, the mentor can share practical strategies that help them overcome the same obstacles. This connection allows the mentor to provide guidance, encouragement, and understanding, which is invaluable for someone struggling to recover. The insights and support from someone who has walked a similar path can make a huge difference.

The key to breaking down those walls and finding the path to healing came from a place where traditional therapy was missing. We needed to give them the belief that they truly could overcome their challenges. We paired them with a personal coach who helped guide them through recovery in a 12-week personal coaching program. Today, Liberating Humanity uses fully immersive guided mediation experiences to help people release a significant part of their trauma in as little as 3-4 days.

PTSD, anxiety, depression, and addictions affect almost everyone in some way. Participating in undercover child rescue missions took an immense emotional toll on many of our operators. After just one mission, many operators chose not to continue due to the weight of what they had witnessed. The burden was tremendous, and I am deeply grateful for every operator who risked everything to help rescue the children. However, the PTSD resulting from these missions often surpassed what our former military personnel experienced in battle. The experiences were heavy, dark, and incredibly challenging. We needed to find a way for the operators to heal from the trauma of their rescue work.

That search for a remedy came when I received a phone call from Jimmy and Andrew, two comrades who had been by my side on over a dozen missions. Andrew's voice carried a hint of mystery as he asked, "Do you trust us?"

"Of course I trust you!" I replied without hesitation. "I've put my life in your hands during our child rescue operations. There isn't anyone I trust more."

"Then you need to join us on something that will change your life this weekend," Jimmy urged.

Jimmy and Andrew were my closest friends, men I trusted completely. Jimmy, fearless to the core, had done everything from running with the bulls to swimming with sharks. I half expected another adrenaline-fueled adventure. But their tone was different this time, thoughtful and compassionate. This wasn't about a thrill; it sounded like something profound that could dramatically improve my life.

Shrouded in mystery, I was intrigued and asked for more details.

"It's a personal transformational event unlike nothing you've ever experienced," Andrew said.

That was a bold statement, considering I had attended every personal development seminar and conference I could find for years. I had walked barefoot across red-hot coals with Tony Robbins. I even broke bricks with my bare hands at an empowerment training course. I had done it all.

"Tell me more," I prodded inquisitively.

They explained how they had met a doctor who had studied various holistic tools to help with anxiety, depression, addictions, PTSD, and other emotional issues. This doctor deeply understood plant medicines and knew how to use them to help people heal from emotional pain.

I began researching the different types of plants the doctor used and discovered that the doctor was working with psychedelics like mushrooms and sassafras. These "plant medicines" had been vilified in the late '60s and classified as Schedule 1 drugs, meaning the US federal government had made them illegal for possession and consumption. Consequently, most people today have been conditioned to believe these plants are as dangerous as cocaine. However, the truth is that they are safer than many over-the-counter medications, with no evidence of addiction or overdose.

I knew a lot about helping people heal from emotional disorders, having built a company dedicated to freeing people from those chains. As I explored deeper into my research, I discovered that Johns Hopkins University had conducted studies on psychedelics with remarkable findings. Not only was there no evidence of residual adverse effects, but when used with a trained facilitator, these substances were also incredibly effective in helping people release childhood trauma, break through addictions, and overcome anxiety and depression.

I joined my fellow operators that weekend for an experience that would change my life—a personal transformation like nothing I had ever encountered. The facilitators not only helped me release the heavy emotional energy from our child rescue experiences, but they also completely changed my view of myself, my life, my relationships, and my connection with God.

Thinking about my transformation, I realize how toxic my past life was, full of material success and destructive behavior. Seeing children being sold changed the direction of my life, making me reevaluate my priorities and fight for those who couldn't defend themselves. However, this guided meditation healing ceremony was a game-changer, helping me let go of my dysfunctional life and guiding me toward forgiveness, self-love, and a higher purpose.

The experience was so profound that I recognized its potential to help those suffering from childhood trauma release their pain more effectively than any of the programs we had used in the past. Inspired by this, we began bringing in professional facilitators specializing in trauma recovery. These experts guided people through processes designed to release deep-seated trauma, offering them new pathways to healing. Participants began to find joy in their lives, experiencing a sense of freedom and peace that had previously seemed unattainable.

These powerful tools must be used with trained facilitators who understand the plants and can create the right environment for healing. The powerful personal transformation benefits of these experiences are not only created from their chemical makeup. Science has proven that a guided, facilitated setting greatly influences positive treatment outcomes.

Another study by Johns Hopkins University found that 75 percent of people who undergo one of these facilitated transformational ceremonies consider it one of the most meaningful and spiritually impactful events of their lives. They also discovered that over two-thirds of people who initially identified as atheists changed their beliefs and became believers in God after only one of these experiences.

In the battle to save the children, we must all look honestly at our own lives and take responsibility for healing our pain. The impact of emotional inheritance is real, whether we acknowledge it or not. Our anxiety and depression can be passed on to our children through their observation of how we react to life. Our addictions directly impact the children around us. Unresolved childhood trauma has the potential to be passed on to our children if we don't seek the support we need to heal ourselves. This is not just a personal journey; it's a generational one, and we each have the power to heal humanity from this pain.

If you or a loved one is struggling with addictions, PTSD, anxiety, depression, or unhealed childhood trauma, realize that there is hope. You do not have to carry this weight alone. Visit us at www. Liberating-Humanity.com to get the resources you need to heal.

Final Words

The pursuit of freedom goes beyond rescuing children from physical captivity. It also means breaking the chains that imprison us all. This collective effort helps us free ourselves from addictions, negative emotions, and past traumas. We all must take responsibility for our own lives and how we contribute to the world around us.

I hope and pray that my experiences liberating children can inspire healing and personal transformation for everyone.

The Sound of Freedom is not just the joyful laughter of rescued children; it is a collective chant echoing through the corridors of human consciousness—a hymn of self-liberation, a symphony of healed souls announcing the beginning of a new era.

Thank you for joining me in the mission of Liberating Humanity.

ACKNOWLEDGMENTS

This journey has been shaped by the many people who have played a crucial role along the way. I am deeply grateful to everyone who has impacted my life and supported this critical mission. Whether through direct action, encouragement, or silent prayers, your support has fueled our fight against child trafficking and our efforts to bring healing and hope to the world. Together, we have forged a strong bond of compassion and courage, and for that, I am profoundly thankful.

First and foremost, I want to express my sincere gratitude to my beloved wife, Hada Vanessa. Her endless love and support have brought me so much joy and happiness. She's always by my side, encouraging me to achieve things I never thought possible. Her belief in me has been a constant source of strength, helping me grow and become more than I ever imagined. This journey wouldn't have been as meaningful or fulfilling without her.

I want to express my deep love for my sweet daughter, Khira, and my three sons, Jordan, Jaden, and Brennan. My greatest hope is to live a life that will make you proud to call me Dad. Every day, I strive to be the kind of father who inspires you and sets an example of courage, integrity, and kindness. I look forward to the day when your children and their children read these stories and feel a deep sense of pride knowing that their grandfather made a meaningful and positive difference in the world. My love for you drives everything I do, and I know that the legacy we build together will inspire future generations.

I am deeply grateful to the former Homeland Security officer who invited me on that mission to Colombia, an invitation that changed the course of my life. Though our paths have since separated, the spark he lit in me set the foundation for everything that came after. His invitation wasn't just a call to action but the start of a journey filled with countless rescue missions and life-altering experiences.

Without that crucial moment, I would never have met the amazing friends who now feel like family or crossed paths with my beloved wife, Hada Vanessa. This work has been more than a mission of justice and compassion; it has also given me some of the greatest joys and relationships of my life. For that, I will always be deeply thankful.

To my friends and fellow operators—Andrew, Jimmy, Joseph, Jeremy, Glenn, Dave, Aaron, J.R., Sean, Brian, Jason, A-Rod, Jason, Ryon, Barry, Radd, Peder, Tixoc, Wiggins, Matt, and Jim. I want to express the profound honor I feel in standing beside you. You are men of unparalleled courage and integrity, willing to descend into the darkest depths of Hell to selflessly protect the innocent. Your bravery is not just in the missions we've undertaken but in the countless sacrifices you've made—sacrifices of time, money, and, most importantly, your very lives and reputations.

You have fought valiantly against the forces of evil, often at significant personal cost, to bring these children to safety. Your unwavering commitment and relentless spirit have made these rescues possible. I honor you not only for what you have done but for the men you are. Each of you is a man of valor, selflessness, and unshakeable resolve. I owe my life to you, and my gratitude for the sacrifices you've made is beyond measure. I will forever be indebted to each of you, and I will always carry the memory of your courage with me.

Each operator who took part in these child rescue missions would not have been able to do so without the unwavering support of their spouses and loving families. Behind every brave operator standing on the front lines is a family providing the strength, encouragement, and love that makes their sacrifice possible. I want to acknowledge the incredible families who stood by these courageous men and women, offering steadfast support in the face of unimaginable challenges.

I am also deeply grateful for the support of my own family—my parents, sisters, and even my former spouses—who have stood by me as I embarked on these dangerous missions. Their belief in the importance of this work and their willingness to accept the risks involved have been a source of strength and comfort. Without their encouragement, I would not have been able to dedicate myself fully to this cause.

To all those who have supported me and my fellow operators in our mission to eradicate child trafficking, I extend my heartfelt thanks. Your love, patience, and understanding have not only made our work possible but have also been a beacon of hope in the darkest of times. You are the unsung heroes of this mission, and I am forever grateful for your sacrifice and support. Together, we have made a difference, and together, we will continue to fight for a world where every child is safe, loved, and free.

A heartfelt thank you goes out to my incredible marketing team and everyone who played a role in bringing this book to life. Josh, Matt, Tyler, and Caroline—your dedication and creativity have been instrumental in sharing this message with the world. I also want to extend my deepest gratitude to the team members who work tirelessly behind the scenes—Jerry, Michelle, and Dave. Your efforts in keeping my life organized have allowed me to focus my energy on the mission that matters most: rescuing children and spreading a message of hope to humanity. Without your support, none of this would have been possible.

I also want to extend a special acknowledgment to the Child Liberation team and everyone who generously donated to this cause. Your heart-centered commitment to this foundation and the children of the world has made an incredible impact. Because of your dedication, safe houses are being built, transformative programs are being implemented, and laws and policies are being rewritten to ensure our children's safety and provide them with the healing they deserve. Your contributions are making a real difference, and for that, I am truly grateful.

Many of these fearless operators continue to work undercover, risking everything to protect the innocent. Others have retired from child rescue operations, yet their impact on the world is far from over. They are now channeling their experiences into building companies and foundations that inspire positive change across humanity.

One story that truly captures the spirit of these remarkable men involves my close friend and fearless operator, Jimmy. Years ago, as he prepared for another undercover mission to rescue children, his then-girlfriend expressed her concerns. "I don't want you to go; this seems really dangerous. Can't THEY do it instead?" she asked. Jimmy's response, reflecting the resolve of the men on our team, was both unyielding and powerful: "We ARE THE THEY!" This realization struck him deeply, reminding him—and all of us—that it's our responsibility to stand up and take bold action to make the world a better place.

Feeling a divine calling, Jimmy became driven to help men everywhere recognize their duty to take charge of their lives and the world around them. This passion led him to create a movement called "We Are The They." This brotherhood unites men on a journey of personal growth, guiding them to discover their power, passion, and purpose. Through his leadership, Jimmy is dedicated to empowering men to become the best versions of themselves, ensuring they leave a lasting, positive mark on the world. His work is a shining example of how one person's courage and conviction can inspire others to step up and make a difference.

About Us

Paul Hutchinson

Paul Hutchinson is more than just a successful business owner, investor, and philanthropist—he is a man driven by a deep, unwavering commitment to making the world a safer place for the most vulnerable among us: our children. Throughout his life, Paul has dedicated himself to creating a world where every child can experience the safety, freedom, and hope they deserve. His work is not just a career; it's a calling that has defined every aspect of his life.

In 2017, Paul channeled this passion into founding the Child Liberation Foundation, an organization that stands as a beacon of hope for countless children trapped in the darkest corners of the world. Paul has personally led or played a crucial role in over seventy undercover rescue missions across fifteen countries. His leadership and dedication have been instrumental in liberating thousands of children from the grips of human trafficking. Through the Child Liberation Foundation and other organizations he helped establish and fund, Paul's efforts have created a ripple effect of freedom and hope, transforming lives and communities around the globe.

Paul's impact doesn't stop there. As the primary investor and Executive Producer of the film Sound of Freedom, Paul brought one of the largest and most significant child rescue missions in history to the world's attention. This powerful film, which highlights the liberation of over 120 victims—an operation in which Paul himself played a pivotal role—serves as both a testament to his courage and a call to action for others to join the fight against child trafficking.

Before dedicating his life to this noble cause, Paul built and sold numerous successful businesses, achieving financial independence and global recognition. In 2017, he retired from his professional career to focus entirely on his philanthropic efforts. His expertise and experience have made him a sought-after keynote speaker, sharing his insights and inspiring action at family office conferences and among royalty and world influencers across the globe.

Paul Hutchinson is respected not only for his extraordinary professional achievements but for the profound and lasting impact he is making in the lives of millions. His tireless dedication to fighting child trafficking and his relentless pursuit of a better world for all children have earned him admiration and recognition worldwide. Through his work, Paul is not just changing lives—he is reshaping the future, one mission, one child at a time.

BOOK PAUL HUTCHINSON FOR YOUR NEXT EVENT

Inspire your audience with a powerful message of courage, leadership, and impact. Paul Hutchinson's firsthand experiences in business, philanthropy, and child rescue make him a dynamic and unforgettable speaker.

Scan the QR code to inquire about booking Paul for your event.

Visit: paulhutchinsonofficial.com/keynote-speaking

Bring a transformative voice to your stage.

THE CHILD LIBERATION FOUNDATION (CLF)

At the Child Liberation Foundation (CLF), we hold a powerful vision: a world where every child feels safe, valued, loved, and nurtured within the embrace of a family. We believe that every child deserves the chance to grow up in an environment that fosters their well-being, free from fear and harm. Our mission is not just to rescue the innocent but to restore hope, dignity, and a sense of belonging to those who have suffered unimaginable abuse.

CLF is dedicated to providing the tools and resources necessary for healing—not only for the children we rescue but also for adults who carry the scars of childhood trauma. We understand that the effects of child sex abuse can last a lifetime, impacting not only the victims but also future generations. That's why our work extends beyond rescue missions; we are committed to breaking the cycle of abuse by empowering survivors to heal and ensuring that the trauma they endured is never passed on.

Our mission is to liberate humanity from the horrors of child sex abuse. This means taking a holistic approach to healing and prevention. We work tirelessly to help victims rebuild their lives, offering them the support they need to overcome their past and reclaim their future. At the same time, we focus on prevention, striving to create a world where no child ever has to experience such pain.

But we can't do it alone. We need your help to make this vision a reality. By joining us, you become a vital part of this mission—a mission to end child sex abuse and bring healing to those who have suffered. Together, we can create a world where every child knows what it means to be safe, cherished, and free. Join us at childliberation.org and be a part of this life-changing work. Your support can help save a child, heal a heart, and change the world.

Scan the QR code to subscribe and stay updated on our work.

Visit: childliberation.org

Together, we can save lives and restore hope.

Liberating Humanity

The mission of Liberating Humanity is to create a world where every individual can live free from the forces that perpetuate pain, division, and suffering. We are dedicated to uprooting the deep-seated issues that plague our society—ranging from generational abuse, PTSD, and addiction to anxiety, depression, and other forms of trauma. Our goal is to break the cycles of despair that hold people back from realizing their full potential and to foster a global community grounded in love, unity, and hope.

Liberating Humanity is not just about addressing the symptoms of societal issues; it's about tackling the root causes head-on. We believe that true liberation begins with healing—healing individuals, families, and communities from the inside out. Our holistic approach encompasses physical, emotional, mental, and spiritual well-being, recognizing that lasting change requires comprehensive solutions.

We are committed to providing the tools and resources necessary for this healing journey. Through our programs, healing retreats, and educational initiatives, we empower people to overcome the obstacles that have held them captive. By raising global consciousness and turning hearts toward compassion, we aim to liberate humanity from the forces of war, division, hatred, envy, fear, and pain.

Our mission extends beyond immediate rescue efforts; it's about prevention and transformation. We strive to create a world where past traumas do not dictate the future, children are safe, and the next generation inherits a world of peace, prosperity, and freedom.

At Liberating Humanity, our mission is encapsulated in three core pillars: Protect, Educate, and Heal. Through these pillars, we work to safeguard the vulnerable, educate the uninformed, and heal the broken, paving the way for a brighter, more unified world. Our vision is bold, our approach is comprehensive, and our commitment is unwavering.

Join us on this transformative journey and learn more about how you can be part of the solution at liberating-humanity.com. Together, we can build a future where every person can thrive in a world of love, unity, and hope.

Scan the QR code to subscribe and become part of the movement.

Visit: liberating-humanity.com

Let's build a future where every person thrives.

APPENDIX

Research shows that using tourniquets before getting to the hospital has a success rate of over 90 percent in controlling severe limb bleeding. National Institutes of Health, severe bleeding, or hemorrhage, is one of the leading causes of preventable death in trauma cases, making up about 40 percent of these deaths. National Library of Medicine: https://www.ncbi.nlm.nih.gov/pmc/articles/PMC6754176.

Charitable Giving Statistics: According to the Giving USA report, Americans donated 1.7 percent of their disposable income to charity in 2022: https://givingusa.org.

Seventy-three percent of child victims do not tell anyone about the abuse for at least a year. Forty-five percent of victims do not tell anyone for at least five years. Some never disclose the abuse they suffered: https://doi.org/10.1080/15374410701279701.

Nearly 70 percent of all reported sexual assaults (including assaults on adults) occur to children ages seventeen and under: http://www.ojp.usdoj.gov/bjs/pub/pdf/saycrle.pdf.

Family structure is the most important risk factor in child sexual abuse. Children living without either parent (foster children) are ten times more likely to be sexually abused than children who live with both biological parents. Children who live with a single parent who has a live-in partner are at the highest risk: they are twenty times more likely to be victims of child sexual abuse than children living with both biological parents: https://cap.law.harvard.edu/wp-content/uploads/2015/07/sedlaknis.pdf.

In a study of over one thousand survivors, the average age at the time of reporting child sex abuse was about fifty-two years: https://childusa.org/wp-content/uploads/2020/04/Delayed-Disclosure-Factsheet-2020.pdf.

About one in four girls and one in twenty boys in the United States experience child sexual abuse. Someone known and trusted by the child or child's family members perpetrates 91 percent of child sexual abuse: https://www.cdc.gov/violenceprevention/childsexualabuse/fastfact.html.

Was a human life worth as little as $200? https://colombiareports.com/colombias-market-price-for-a-life.

The majority of perpetrators were once victims themselves: Overall, **68 percent** of the incarcerated adult male felons reported some form of early childhood victimization. National Institute of Justice: https://www.ojp.gov/pdffiles/fs000204.pdf.

Alarmingly, 25 percent of Haitian children aged 5–17 are separated from their biological parents, leading lives filled with hardship and despair: https://en.wikipedia.org/wiki/Restavek.

This disturbing practice reflects the darkest aspects of modern-day slavery and child trafficking, with an estimated 300,000 Haitian children trapped in such conditions: https://en.wikipedia.org/wiki/Slavery_in_Haiti.

Between 30–40 percent of people who are abused as children become abusers themselves. Source: https://www.theguardian.com/society/2013/sep/17/breaking-the-cycle-of-abuse.

26 percent of adults in the United States—about one in four—suffer from a diagnosable mental disorder: https://www.hopkinsmedicine. org/health/wellness-and-prevention/mental-health-disorder-statistics.

Approximately 10 percent of all organ transplants involve trafficked organs. National Library of Medicine: https://www.ncbi.nlm.nih. gov/pmc/articles/PMC4946496.

PSYCHEDELICS RESEARCH

Johns Hopkins University studies, 75 percent of people rank the experience as among the most meaningful and spiritually significant in their lifetime: https://hub.jhu.edu/2019/04/26/ experiencing-god-psychedelics-mental-health.

The powerful personal transformation benefits of psychedelics are not merely derived from their pharmacology. Science has proven that positive treatment outcomes are influenced in large part by the guided, facilitated setting itself: https://journals.sagepub.com/ doi/10.1177/0269881118754710.

Psilocybin is one of the safest tools for the release of anxiety, depression, addictions, and PTSD. There is no evidence of post-acute adverse effects: https://pubmed.ncbi.nlm.nih.gov/33143790.

www.ingramcontent.com/pod-product-compliance
Lightning Source LLC
Chambersburg PA
CBHW071325120626
46546CB00002B/440